■SCHOLASTIC

D1122096

Differentiated Literacy Centers

Margo Southall

New York • Toronto • London • Auckland • Sydney
Mexico City • New Delhi • Hong Kong • Buenos Aires

Teaching *Resources*

This book is dedicated to my mother, Barbara Lea Taylor, a fellow writer, whose poetic fluency continues to be an inspiration to me.

I would also like to thank Mildred Nelson, Phyllis Phillips and the teachers of Metropolitan Nashville Public Schools for their constructive feedback and collegial support at the many literacy centers workshops, who recognized the need and helped develop the format for this book.

To my editors, thank you for persevering through the mountain of center activities in my initial drafts to bring this book forward in such a teacher-friendly format.

Finally, a thank you to my family for your understanding of the time I have needed to devote to my research and writing.

Copy editor: Carol Ghiglieri
Cover design: Brian LaRossa
Interior design: Kelli Thompson

ISBN-13: 978-0-439-89909-3
ISBN-10: 0-439-89909-5

Contents

CHAPTER 1

Introduction to Differentiated Literacy Centers

To open this book, I begin with a bit of a confession—I was not always successful at structuring my literacy centers to best support all of my students. It took a close look at the center activities I assigned, the procedures I expected students to follow, and my teaching around the center work before I understood how my "one-size-fits-all" approach was leaving some students unsupported and others unchallenged. This book is the result of years of changes that helped me create a literacy center program that truly supports standards-based reading and writing instruction and meets student needs. It is my intention that this guide helps you to create both an effective and easy-to-manage centers program that supports each and every student on his or her literacy journey.

How Much Time Were My Students Actually Reading and Writing at Literacy Centers?

Students are often off-task when center activities are not differentiated.

Scenario 1:

Brittney at My Traditional Literacy Centers

5 minutes: Brittney stands by the shelf of book tubs, picks up the book *More Spaghetti, I Say* from the H tub, puts it back, picks up another book. Then she repeats this with two more selections. Brittney finds a chair at the Reading Center area.

4 minutes: Brittney flips through her book and then reads it.

2 minutes: She looks at what the others in her team are doing and asks Tamika what they are supposed to do when they've read their book. Tamika points to the form in the tray.

3 minutes: Brittney takes a form, looks at it, and then looks at the sheet that Jayden is writing on next to her. She draws a picture.

4 minutes: She begins to talk to Jayden, asking him if he likes her picture and continues talking off-topic.

1 minute: Brittney begins to copy Jayden's writing, but he tells her she should be writing about her own book.

1 minute: She begins to write "I like . . . " and stops as the signal sounds for tidy-up time.

Total Minutes: 20   **Reading: 4**   **Writing: 1**   **On Task: 9** (includes selection of materials)

Where It All Began

Our school literacy team was examining ways to increase the time students were reading and writing each day in our classrooms. We already had 150 minutes dedicated to literacy instruction each day: sixty of these were allotted for teacher-managed small-group instruction alongside student-managed literacy centers; the remaining time was devoted to read-alouds, shared reading, word study (decoding and spelling), and writer's workshop. Surely we offered our students ample opportunity for extended periods of reading and writing each day! Our observations and assessment of students in small-group instruction demonstrated that this instructional time was well spent, but we questioned just how many minutes our students were actually engaged in reading and writing at the literacy centers while we worked with those groups. Were we maximizing this time for student-driven learning?

To determine whether this was the case in my own classroom, I decided to block off one day of small-group instruction so that I could observe and track the number of minutes a specific student spent engaged in reading and writing. For this purpose, I chose one of my struggling readers, Brittney. You read the summary of this observation in Scenario 1. But Brittney wasn't an anomaly. Further observations showed that many of my students were having trouble managing their time and completing their work during literacy centers. I discovered that students were:

- spending more time browsing the reading materials than reading them.
- unsure how to respond to their reading.
- drawing and talking off-task.
- depending on directions from and/or copying the work of other group members.

Comfort Zone Meets the Zone of Proximal Development

This lack of productivity was not what I had envisioned for the literacy centers in my classroom. I realized that behind the management challenge was an instructional one: students with more advanced literacy skills were completing activities in their comfort zone, while struggling students were not able to keep up. Few students were working in their zone of proximal development, the level of challenge at which learning takes place (Vygotsky, 1978). The more advanced students were *not getting the challenge they needed to grow and my struggling readers were leaving tasks unfinished, or relying on their peers* to "get them through" the activities without developing an understanding. Either way, they were not maximizing their literacy center time, and this was precious learning time that none of us could afford to waste.

I was familiar with the concept of tiered assignments in which the same task is presented at varying levels of challenge to ensure success for all students. Why could I not use the same data I used to guide my small-group instruction to plan tiered activities for my literacy centers so they would be more closely aligned with student need? The direction was clear, but I wasn't sure how to make this manageable, given an already overloaded work schedule. The challenge was to plan and prepare multilevel activities for the literacy skills I was teaching, in a way that would be sustainable throughout the year. I set out on a creative journey (the part I do so love as a teacher), and the culmination is the book you hold in your hands.

The Florida Center for Reading Research defines differentiated instruction as "matching instruction to meet the different needs of learners in a given classroom that includes small groups and increased practice opportunities in the form of reading centers." (2006)

Differentiated Literacy Centers in Action

Scenario 2:

Brittney at My Redesigned Differentiated Literacy Centers

2 minutes: Brittney takes her book box from the bookshelf. She walks to the Comprehension Center area, takes a seat, and looks around at the other team members.

4 minutes: Brittney reads her book *Robert and the Rocket*.

1 minute: She picks up the green-colored (beginning level) task card with picture-cued sentence starters and reads the prompts.

1 minute: Brittney chews the top of her pencil for a moment. She flips through the pages of her book again, looking at the pictures.

Time spent reading and writing dramatically increases when activities are differentiated.

3 minutes: She writes a sentence in her centers notebook "I see . . . "

1 minute: Brittney stops writing and looks at the card with sentence cues again.

3 minutes: Brittney writes a second sentence "I wonder . . ."

1 minute: She reads her writing to herself.

4 minutes: Brittney asks Jayden if he will be her thinking partner, reads her sentences to him, talks about a part she has read, and shows him a picture in the book. Then she listens to Jayden read his questions about *Shipwreck Saturday* and they talk about the story.

Total Minutes: 20   Reading: 7   Writing: 5   On-Task: 17

What's the difference between Scenarios 1 and 2? Nearly double the time spent reading and so much more time spent writing! Time on-task increased dramatically when Brittney was provided with the following:

- Her own box of reading materials at her independent level, selected during morning routines and during guided reading. *Students now spent more time actually reading and responding during center time because they were able to focus on a few preselected books, rather than browsing leisurely through book tubs.* By having these books ready to go, Brittney was ready to go, too.

Student book boxes containing independent level text provide a source of ready-to-go reading materials.

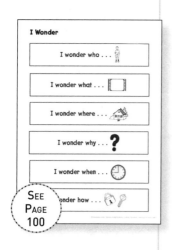

SEE PAGE 100

- Picture-cued differentiated tasks that supported her response to the reading. *Often the hardest part for my struggling students is getting started—writing those first words. The picture-cued, open-ended sentence starters made a huge difference in helping students like Brittney produce a focused response— and giving more advanced readers the opportunity to engage in a higher-level response.*

- Teacher modeling along with ample opportunity for students to discuss their understanding of a strategy. I *began to integrate pair-share activities throughout the day during read-alouds, shared reading, and classroom discussion of content material. Oral discussion of the reading became an important element of the literacy centers, as well.* Expressing her ideas aloud and responding to the questions and comments of her peers during center time was critical to Brittney's success in processing her learning. (See Providing an Appropriate Level of Support in Chapter 2 for more on this topic.)

We know that in order to close the achievement gap for students like Brittney, it is critical that they receive ample explicit instruction and time to engage in authentic reading and writing. When we make fundamental changes, such as the ones above, to our literacy centers, the amount and quality of reading and writing practice increases dramatically, taking students who struggle much farther along the path to literacy, while also helping their more skilled peers push ahead.

How Does Differentiation Work With Literacy Centers?

To achieve the changes demonstrated in Scenario 2, I had to do some strategic planning and restructuring of my original literacy centers. The differentiated literacy centers (DLCs) I developed contain reading and writing activities that directly support whole-class and small-group instruction. Each center offers multilevel literacy activities that are assigned to individuals and groups of students based on their demonstrated (data-based) need in order to strengthen specific skills and strategies. Differentiated center tasks also take into account student interests and the level of support students require in order to complete their literacy assignments; see Table 1.1 for a comparison of differentiated learning centers and traditional ones. The ultimate goal of DLCs is to support an easy-to-manage, success-oriented literacy program.

"Differentiation involves responsive teaching and scaffolding students' learning . . . When you differentiate instruction you operate with the premise that all children learn at different paces and in different ways . . . Our curriculum tells us what to teach, but it is differentiation that guides us in how to teach."
(Drapeau, 2004)

What's Different About Differentiated Literacy Centers?	
Traditional Literacy Centers	Differentiated Literacy Centers
• Activities are based on whole-class instruction.	• Activities are based on student assessment data.
• Differentiated resources are not available.	• Students work with multilevel resources.
• Students may become bored or frustrated.	• Students are engaged in their learning.
• Individual levels of support are not part of the center design.	• Levels of support based on student need are incorporated into the design of each center.
• One level of response is provided for each activity.	• Tiered activities include varied responses for each skill or strategy.
• Students may select activities that are outside their instructional zone.	• Students follow a simple coding system to select activities within their instructional zone.

The Structure of DLCs

We begin with setting up three core, yearlong centers that develop skills in the key literacy areas: comprehension, fluency, and word study (phonemic awareness, phonics, high-frequency words and vocabulary), as shown below.

Three Core Literacy Centers	
Center	**Purpose**
Reading Comprehension	Students will: • Practice and apply modeled comprehension strategies during independent reading of leveled text • Demonstrate understanding of skills and strategies using multilevel responses • Deepen their comprehension through writing in response to reading
Fluency	Students will: • Develop fluent reading strategies using independent-level text • Increase reading accuracy, rate, use of expression, and meaningful phrasing during oral reading • Participate in repeated readings within collaborative and self-monitoring formats
Word Study	Students will: • Acquire an understanding of how words work through multisensory practice and the use of tactile materials • Transfer phonics skills to reading and spelling new single-syllable and multisyllabic words • Achieve automaticity in recognizing and spelling irregular high-frequency words

Next, we make sure that these centers reach the range of learners in our classrooms. The resources in the following chapters help you develop a menu of tasks that vary in difficulty for each of the three core centers. Being familiar with both the multilevel activities and the materials they require is key to your success—these are described briefly in the next section.

Multilevel Center Activities

Multilevel center activities are strategy-based tasks designed at three levels of challenge: beginner, intermediate, and advanced. By using these tiered center activities, teachers enable students with different learning needs to apply the same key skills and strategies but at varying levels of complexity and open-endedness (Tomlinson, 1999). For example, three students at the comprehension center may all work on a questioning activity, yet each one will be reading a different leveled text and completing an activity page that has been designed to meet his or her needs, based on assessment.

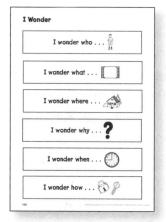

Beginner

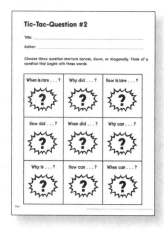

Intermediate

Advanced

Students work on the same questioning strategies but complete tasks that are appropriate to their skill level.

Differentiated Literacy Center Materials

Reading materials, activity sheets, graphic organizers, and other learning materials such as word cards all need to be differentiated for the three levels of activities. Reading materials should be provided at each student's independent reading level (95–100 percent accuracy rate for fiction, 97–100 percent for nonfiction). You can select from the alternative task cards, student prompts, recording forms, and suggested manipulative materials in the following chapters to meet the needs of students who struggle with reading or require additional support with organizational skills. In this way, you can modify tasks while still allowing students to participate in the same activity as their peers. These modifications maintain students' self-esteem and support their engagement and motivation.

How Do Differentiated Literacy Centers Support My Instruction?

The three core centers address the essential skills and strategies as identified by the National Reading Panel (2000). These include phonemic awareness, phonics, fluency, vocabulary, and comprehension (see page 10 for an overview of the centers). Differentiated literacy centers are part of the daily instructional cycle as we assess, plan, and implement instruction according to our curriculum. They provide opportunities for students to practice skills and strategies at their level and based on their needs. The figure below illustrates how DLCs can support your daily instruction.

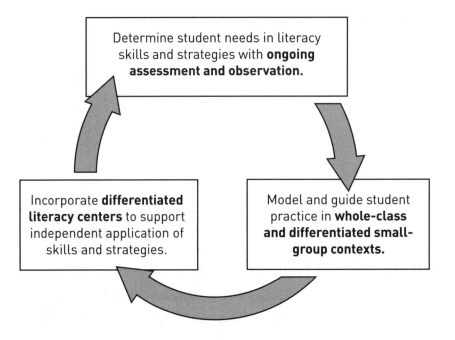

Determine student needs in literacy skills and strategies with **ongoing assessment and observation.**

Model and guide student practice in **whole-class and differentiated small-group contexts.**

Incorporate **differentiated literacy centers** to support independent application of skills and strategies.

A differentiated classroom meets the learners at the point of need on a continuum of literacy learning and provides developmentally appropriate learning activities based upon ongoing assessment and an understanding of how our students learn. By using the organizational guidelines for determining student need provided in Chapter 2, together with the center resources included in the following chapters, you will be able to implement a differentiated literacy center program that addresses demonstrated student needs within a multilevel classroom. In this way, every student may be both challenged and supported within a differentiated instructional framework.

How do you pull together differentiated literacy centers, remain sane, and have a life outside of school? Here is my advice—discussed in detail in the coming chapters—for maintaining your sanity:

Select sustainable formats and activities; avoid the one-time wonders ("I'm done!"). (Chapters 3 through 6)

Address the needs of every student with multilevel tasks. (Chapter 2)

Never add a center activity without teacher modeling and guided student practice. (Chapters 3, 4 through 6)

Include activities designed to support the literacy skills you teach (whole class, small group). (Chapters 2, 4 through 6)

Track center work with a simple system and hold students accountable. (Chapters 2 and 3)

Follow these steps, and . . .

You will make differentiated instruction a reality without adding to your workload!

CHAPTER 2

Planning Literacy Centers to Meet Student Needs

The Differentiated Learning Triangle below represents three key sources of information that empower us to strategically differentiate our literacy centers based on demonstrated student needs and strengths: assessment data, the level of support students require in order to successfully complete a center task, and the profile of the student as a learner. This chapter helps you use the three-point framework to determine the center activities that will be most effective for your students at each stage of their literacy development.

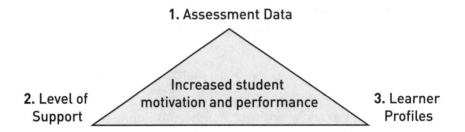

The Differentiated Learning Triangle: Information That Drives an Effective Literacy Program

Assessment data is the first point that drives instruction. We use formal and informal assessment data on students' reading performance to decide which comprehension, fluency, and word study center activities to offer (see Assessment Data, pages 15–31). However, assessment data alone are not sufficient to tap students' individual strengths and address their areas of weakness. We also need to know how much support students require within the classroom environment in order to successfully complete a task.

The **level of support** you provide for students' learning—the second point of the triangle—is discussed in detail on pages 32–37. I describe ways to scaffold learning tasks with peer and teacher support so that every child can grasp and use the literacy skills they need in order to read and write successfully in literacy centers and beyond.

The third point of the triangle is the **profile of the student** as a learner. The last section of this chapter (pages 37–43) helps you build learning profiles for your students. You'll want to gather the following information in detail—especially for your struggling or disengaged learners: What is the student's attitude toward reading, spelling, and writing? Which types of activities and topics engage and motivate this learner? What aptitudes has he or she demonstrated that could be tapped further using Gardner's (1993) theory of multiple intelligences?

Together, these three sources of information in the Differentiated Learning Triangle provide us with a guide to selecting center activity options along with the specific level of center task (Beginner, Intermediate, Advanced) that are most appropriate for our students.

Assessment Data: The Key to Well-Planned Centers

Multiple studies have demonstrated that the rate of student achievement is increased when we differentiate our instruction according to the data-based performance of our students (Pressley et al., 2001; Allington, 2005). In this section I recommend assessment tools and ways to use the results to select the appropriate center activities.

Ongoing Informal Assessment

Identifying the center activities and level of challenge that will be most appropriate for our students requires ongoing assessment of their needs. For the classroom teacher, the central question remains, which assessment tools are the most informative and teacher-friendly in terms of the time they take to administer? Walpole and McKenna (2006) have worked extensively in this area and recommend a list of informal assessments. These are correlated to the literacy centers in the following chart:

"Frequent monitoring of student progress increases student achievement and decreases the number of students reading below grade level. Informal classroom-based assessment is used to inform instruction and monitor student progress." (Dole, 2004)

Differentiated Literacy Centers	Informal Assessments
Word Study *Phonemic awareness* *Phonics* *Vocabulary*	• All levels of phonological awareness and phoneme segmentation • Letter-name and letter-sound inventory • Phonics inventory • Pseudo-word decoding test • Developmental spelling inventory • Graded word lists • High-frequency-word reading and spelling test
Fluency *Oral Reading*	• Graded passages to assess accuracy and rate • Rubric for evaluating prosody
Comprehension *Strategy Use*	• Retelling rubric • Questions based on narrative and informational text
All Centers	• Reading motivation interview and survey

Planning Differentiated Literacy Centers Based on Assessment Data

The information from these or other assessments you are currently using will provide the information you need to identify the center activities that best meet the needs of your students. As you determine the needs of students in the areas of comprehension, fluency, and word study, notice which students require more extensive practice opportunities and which skills or strategies they seem to be struggling with. This will guide your use of each of the center planning forms in this chapter.

To plan and record the activities you will provide at each center during a specific center rotation or unit (see Chapter 3 for ways to rotate groups through centers), review each of the four steps below. Likely, you will have one or more students whose learning needs require that you look in more detail at each aspect of the Differentiated Literacy Triangle in order to plan responsive teaching. The fourth step is designed for this purpose. I use the companion support form (Integrating Sources of Information) for my own planning and as a basis for discussion during our regularly scheduled intervention team meetings so that we can identify how best to teach, support, and engage this student.

Four Steps to Differentiated Centers

1. **Identify the Appropriate Level of Challenge for Your Students**

   Examine the criteria for the three levels of challenge (Beginner, Intermediate, and Advanced) on the Determining the Level of Challenge form for each center (comprehension, page 22; fluency, page 26; word study, page 29). Use student assessment data to determine the performance level indicated for each of the three levels of challenge.

Differentiated Centers: Step by Step

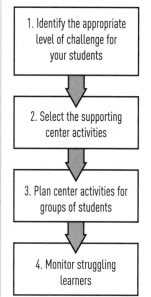

1. Identify the appropriate level of challenge for your students

2. Select the supporting center activities

3. Plan center activities for groups of students

4. Monitor struggling learners

Determining the Level of Challenge: Comprehension Center			
Skill/Strategy	**Beginner Level**	**Intermediate Level**	**Advanced Level**
Making Connections	Does not make connections to the text	Talks about what text reminds him/her of, but cannot explain how it relates to the text	Relates background knowledge and experience to the text
Questioning.	unable to ask or answer questions; gives off-topic responses	Begins to ask and answer questions, but is unable to support them with evidence from the text	Asks and answers questions and is beginning to provi evidence from t

SEE PAGE 22

2. **Select the Supporting Center Activities**

   Refer to the Aligning Student Need and Center Activities chart to select activities for each center that directly support the skills and strategies students most need to practice and extend at this time (comprehension, pages 23–24; fluency, page 27; word study, pages 30–31).

Aligning Student Need and Center Activities: Comprehension Center			
WHEN the student requires practice in	**THEN provide these literacy center activities**	**Challenge Level**	**Page Number**
Making Connections and Self-Monitoring:			
• Connecting their prior experience to the story elements or information on the topic contained within illustrations	• What Do I See? What Do I Know?	B	80
• Responding emotionally and intellectually to the ideas, events or information in the text	• Read, Relate , Respond • Connection Stems • What I Think	M B I	79 80 81
• Self-monitoring for understanding	• In the Driver's Seat	I	82
• Integrating all three levels of connections during reading (self, text, world)	• Build a Connection • Tic-Tac-Connect	A A	

SEE PAGE 23

3. Plan Center Activities for Groups of Students

Plan and track the activities for groups of students who will be working on the same skills and at the same level of challenge at the centers. On the form Planning a Unit of Differentiated Literacy Centers for Groups of Students (page 19), list the center activities for each level of challenge and alongside these note the names of the students participating in each. This information will provide you with a quick reference guide for preparing and displaying the center activities for a single rotation or unit. To save time, print the names in each group on adhesive labels and place these in the second column for students.

Planning a Unit of Differentiated Literacy Centers for Groups of Students

Comprehension Center

Beginner Activities:	Students:		
❑ Read, Relate, Respond	Selena	Devin	Keshondra
❑ Connection Stems	James	Brittney	
❑			

Intermediate Activities:	Students:			
❑ What I Think	Dylan	Tamika	David	Antwain
❑ In the Driver's Seat	Jacob	Courtney	Eunicia	Lamar
❑	Makayla	Jermaine		

Advanced Activities:	Students:		
❑ Build a Connection	Antonio	Kayla	Raho
❑ Tic Tac Connect	Justin	Celeste	
❑			

Fluency Center

Beginner Activities:	Students:	
❑ Read Along and Respond	Selena	Devin
❑ Froggy Phrases	James	

SEE PAGE 19

**Integrating Sources of Information:
Planning for a Differentiated Program**

Differentiated Learning Triangle	Word Study	Fluency	Comprehension
Student: Brittney **Date:** September 20	Where is the student developmentally in his or her understanding of how words work? Does the student apply his/her understanding of spelling features to reading and writing contexts? Does the student recognize and spell high-frequency words with accuracy?	Does he/she read: With accuracy? Too slowly? Too quickly? In meaningful phrases? With expression?	Does the student apply modeled strategies during independent reading? Does the student generate and answer literal- and higher-level questions about what he or she has read? Can the student retell what he or she has read orally? In writing?
Assessment Data: Sources of information that guide the practice at the centers Areas of instructional focus at this time based on data	Analysis of Running Records, Developmental Spelling Analysis, phonics inventory, Fry's sight word test, writing samples Coaching for application of modeled word-solving strategies during reading; Word building; sorting to support recognition of words with short vowel patterns; multisensory sight word practice	1-minute timed reading. Fluency Rubric Recognition of sight word phrases Increase pace of reading and the use of intonation with repeated reading of familiar poems, character lines, short passages	Running Record retelling, Comprehension strategy rubric, Reading response notebook Retell the key events in a story Respond to questions using events or information in the text
Level of Support: Level of support the student requires in the learning environment	Additional teacher and peer modeling of routines and activities at the center Center partner Manipulatives and word lists	Tape-Assisted Reading, Read Along Chart, partner or group format for repeated practice of expressive reading	Picture cues of story elements to manipulate in order as she retells Short, highly structured text (12-16 pages) with illustration support
Learner Profile: Center activities and materials that reflect the strengths and interests of the learner	Magic Mat Mix and Fix (with magnetic board and letters) Word Games	Froggy Phrase Slide Get the Beat (with feedback phone) Partner reading	Retelling Cube for Stories and Summary Cube for Facts Picture Question Cards for partner retelling and generating questions independently

Differentiated Literacy Centers © 2007 by Margo Southall, Scholastic Teaching

SEE PAGE 20

4. Monitor Struggling Learners

When planning for individual students who are not reading at grade level and/or require a more in-depth analysis of their specific learning needs, use the Integrating Sources of Information form (page 20). This form helps you summarize the results of recent assessment data, reflect on the level of support the student requires to complete daily tasks (What is working for this student?), plan center activities that allow the student to demonstrate his or her understanding in a way that ensures success, and provide materials that help the student remain engaged in learning.

Planning a Unit of Differentiated Literacy Centers for Groups of Students

_____ Center

Beginner Activities: ❏ ❏ ❏	Students:
Intermediate Activities: ❏ ❏ ❏	Students:
Advanced Activities: ❏ ❏ ❏	Students:
Multilevel Activities: ❏ ❏	Students:

_____ Center

Beginner Activities: ❏ ❏ ❏	Students:
Intermediate Activities: ❏ ❏ ❏	Students:
Advanced Activities: ❏ ❏ ❏	Students:
Multilevel Activities: ❏ ❏	Students:

Integrating Sources of Information:
Planning for a Differentiated Program

Differentiated Learning Triangle	Word Study	Fluency	Comprehension
Student: **Date:**	Where is the student developmentally in his or her understanding of how words work? Does the student apply his/her understanding of spelling features to reading and writing contexts? Does the student recognize and spell high-frequency words with accuracy?	Does he/she read: With accuracy? Too slowly? Too quickly? In meaningful phrases? With expression?	Does the student apply modeled strategies during independent reading? Does the student generate and answer literal and higher-level questions about what he or she has read? Can the student retell what he or she has read orally? In writing?
Assessment Data: Sources of information that guide the practice at the centers Areas of instructional focus at this time based on data			
Level of Support: Level of support the student requires in the learning environment			
Learner Profile: Center activities and materials that reflect the strengths and interests of the learner			

Differentiated Literacy Centers © 2007 by Margo Southall, Scholastic Teaching Resources page 20

Use Planning Forms as an Ongoing Guide for Center Rotations

By compiling these forms in a center planning notebook, you will be able to easily review the number of times students have practiced a specific skill/strategy and the level of challenge and then use this information to plan the next rotation of centers. If students have achieved a satisfactory level of performance with a specific skill/strategy then you will either move them to the next level of challenge for this skill/strategy or move on to the next skill in your literacy program. Many core reading programs provide a scope and sequence of skills and strategies. By reviewing this guide and your assessment data, you will be able to determine the next focus for the center practice activities.

Comprehension Center

The comprehension center activities are organized into four strategy areas: Making Connections and Self-Monitoring, Generating and Answering Questions, Retelling and Summarizing, and Evaluating and Determining Importance. To ensure that students will be engaged and able to work independently at this center, the reading materials must correspond to a student's independent reading level (95–100 percent accuracy). Students will read their independent text and refer to the directions at the center to respond either orally, in writing, with a graphic organizer, or through drawing (see Chapter 4).

Assessing Comprehension

To determine students' reading levels, informal assessment tools, such as Informal Reading Inventories (IRI), or running records, are commonly used. To gain a more in-depth assessment of comprehension at specific times during the year, assessments such as J. John's Informal Reading Inventory (8th edition, Kendall-Hunt), Qualitative Reading Inventory (Leslie & Caldwell, 2005, 4th edition, Allyn & Bacon) or the Scholastic Reading Inventory are also very useful, as they require students not only to retell the events or information but also demonstrate their understanding of the text through the integration of multiple comprehension strategies.

Some students are very good at regurgitating information or a series of events and responding to literal-level questions without

Planning Each Center in Detail
Chapters 4, 5, and 6 provide more background on planning for each of the three core centers, as well as all the procedures and companion reproducibles for activities listed in this chapter.

applying critical-thinking skills. It is important that the assessments you use incorporate higher-level questions and are based on the reading of both fiction and informational text to gain greater insight into the strategies a student is able to apply to the text. Assessment of comprehension strategy use and data-driven instruction ensures that students do not simply move through a progression of leveled texts based on their ability to decode; they must also show that they are acquiring the strategies essential for comprehension as well.

The Determining the Level of Challenge form (below) provides a reference for determining the next steps for student comprehension practice at the centers. The Aligning Student Need chart (at right) provides a list of activities aligned with each of the comprehension strategies, identified by the level of challenge. Determine which of the areas of comprehension practice is a priority for your students at this time, and list the corresponding activities on the Planning a Unit of Differentiated Literacy Centers for Groups of Students chart (page 19).

Determining the Level of Challenge: Comprehension Center			
Skill/Strategy	Beginner Level	Intermediate Level	Advanced Level
Making Connections and Self-Monitoring	Does not make connections to the text	Talks about what text reminds him/her of, but cannot explain how it relates to the text	Relates background knowledge and experience to the text
Questioning.	Is unable to ask or answer questions; gives off-topic responses	Begins to ask and answer questions, but is unable to support them with evidence from the text	Asks and answers questions and is beginning to provide evidence from the text
Retelling and Summarizing.	Is unable to retell story elements or information from the text	Retells some elements of the text; events or information may not be sequential	Retells all story elements or key ideas/concepts from the text in a logical sequence
Evaluating and Determining Importance	Draws no conclusions; does not express opinions or connect the text to his/her ideas and beliefs	Draws conclusions; expresses opinions; is unable to explain the reasoning or connect the text to his/her ideas and beliefs	Draws conclusions; expresses opinions; makes some attempt to explain the reasoning and/or connect the text to his/her ideas and beliefs

Aligning Student Need and Center Activities: Comprehension Center

WHEN the student requires practice in	THEN provide these literacy center activities	Challenge Level	Page Number
Making Connections and Self-Monitoring:			
• Connecting their prior experience to the story elements or information on the topic contained within illustrations	• What Do I See? What Do I Know?	B	80
• Responding emotionally and intellectually to the ideas, events or information in the text	• Read, Relate , Respond • Connection Stems • What I Think	M B I	79 80 81
• Self-monitoring for understanding	• In the Driver's Seat	I	82
• Integrating all three levels of connections during reading (self, text, world)	• Build a Connection • Tic-Tac-Connect	A A	82 83
Generating and Answering Questions:			
• Asking who, what, where, when, why & how questions	• Partner Quiz	M	92
• Generating open-ended questions using a question stem	• I Wonder	B	93
• Generating questions that focus on the character or topic	• Who or What Am I?	B	94
• Generating questions based upon visual information	• I See, I Wonder	B	93
• Asking questions based on new information in the text	• Questions and Answers • Tic-Tac-Question #1	I I	96 96
• Interacting with the text and recording questions during reading	• Sticky Questions	I	94
• Generating and answering literal, inferential, and evaluative questions	• Tic-Tac-Question #2, #3 • Roll Up A Question • What Kinds of Questions Do They Ask?	I, A I A	96,97 98 97

Key: B = Beginner, I = Intermediate, A = Advanced, M = Multilevel

Aligning Student Need and Center Activities: Comprehension Center

WHEN the student requires practice in	THEN provide these literacy center activities	Challenge Level	Page Number
Retelling and Summarizing:			
• Retelling the central elements of a story (character, setting, sequence of events, problem, solution)	• Stop, Draw, and Write • Retelling Flap Book • Retelling Cube for Stories • Tic-Tac-Tell for Stories • Pyramid Summary	M B B I A	108 108 109 110 111
• Identifying key actions, dialogue and thoughts of the character	• Character Close Up	I	116
• Retelling the information in nonfiction text and identifying new information they have learned	• Retelling Cube for Facts • Tic-Tac-Tell for Facts • Roll and Respond Cube • Pyramid Summary	B I A A	109 111 112 111
• Orally summarizing fiction and nonfiction reading material	• Partner Quiz Cards	A	112
Evaluating:			
• Considering the merit in the author's writing (ideas, content) and identifying possibilities for extending or revising this further	• Talk to the Author • Star Review	B I	123 125
• Critiquing the author's use of techniques to establish a hook to the book, provide an engaging series of events, and close with a satisfying ending	• Readers' Café	B	124
• Identifying important events, facts and words	• What's Most Important?	I	125
• Considering the merit in the author's writing; evaluating the author's purpose, audience, and ways in which this text could be used	• Reason to Read • Critic's Cube	M A	123 126

Key: B = Beginner, I = Intermediate, A = Advanced, M = Multilevel

Fluency Center

The fluency center activities are organized into four categories: Fluency With Words, Fluency With Phrases, Fluency With Connected Text, and Technology-Assisted Reading. Note that "connected text" often takes the form of stories, songs, and poems that have been read to and with the students several times during shared reading so that the student can now read them at an independent level. When unfamiliar reading materials are used at the center without supports such as taped versions or digital text, they need to reflect the range of individual reading levels in your classroom, or your students' primary focus will be on decoding (see Resources for multilevel materials at the end of Chapter 5).

Assessing Fluency

One-minute timed readings are commonly used for assessing student accuracy and rate of reading. Informal reading inventories and running records are also useful not only to identify the appropriate level of text for fluency practice, but also, when timed, to determine the fluency rate. Both of these assessment tools can yield important information regarding the other aspects of fluency when analyzed for evidence of meaningful phrasing and the use of expression. For example, while taking a running record, the teacher may make notations on the number and length of student pauses during reading, mark groups of words that were read together as a phrase, and circle punctuation marks that were not observed.

Fluency rubrics, such the NAEP Fluency Scale in Timothy Rasinski's book *The Fluent Reader* (Scholastic, 2003), provide information on the student's progression from reading word by word to multiple-word phrases and his or her use of expression, intonation, and pace.

The Determining the Level of Challenge form (page 26) helps you focus on similar aspects of fluency and gauge the current skill levels of your students. The Aligning Student Need chart (page 27) lists the goals for fluency instruction alongside the center activities that provide student practice. As you listen to your students read, you will be able to determine which of the areas of fluency practice are a priority for your students at this time, and list the corresponding activities on the planning chart.

Self-Assessment
Opportunities for self-monitoring and peer feedback based on specific criteria are provided in the Tell a Tape and Fluency Feedback forms for partner reading (see Chapter 5).

Determining the Level of Challenge: Fluency Center			
Skill/Strategy	**Beginner Level**	**Intermediate Level**	**Advanced Level**
Word Recognition Rate (decodable and high-frequency words)	Hesitates on many of the words	Hesitates on some words	Rarely hesitates on words
Phrasing (Phrase and Connected Text)	Reads word by word; does not recognize phrase boundaries; author's meaning may not be preserved	Reads mostly in two- or three-word phrases; some word-by-word reading and choppiness	Reads in meaningful phrases of three to four words; maintains author's sentence structure and meaning
Pace (Words, Phrases, and Connected Text)	Reads at a slow, laborious pace	Mixture of slow and faster reading	Conversational style of reading; pace is appropriate to the context
Intonation (Phrases and Connected Text)	Reading is monotone, little or no expression or intonation; does not attend to punctuation cues	Some of the text is read with expression and intonation; may exhibit inappropriate use of stress	Most of text is read with appropriate expression and intonation

Word Study Center

The word study center activities are organized into four categories: Alphabet Recognition and Letter-Sound Relationships, Vowel Patterns, High-Frequency Words, and Compounds and Affixes. In any one classroom there will be students who represent a wide range of word knowledge. There is a reciprocal relationship between reading and spelling and a child's decoding skills. As I listen to my students read and analyze their running records, I consider the spelling features they know and apply as they read and the ones that cause them to hesitate and make substitutions or omissions. Their strengths and needs in decoding skills and recognition of sight words, together with their developmental spellings, inform my programming at the word study center. Typically, students are able to read more words than they can accurately spell because when reading they have the support of context cues. Students may decode specific categories of words fluently and recognize irregular high-frequency words in print, yet their spellings demonstrate that they do not have a complete visual memory for these letter sequences.

Aligning Student Need and Center Activities: Fluency Center

WHEN the student requires practice in	THEN provide these literacy center activities	Level of Challenge	Page Number
Fluency With Words			
• Increasing accuracy and speed in reading words	• Word Reading Relay	M	138
• Recognizing familiar spelling patterns and high frequency words)	• Partner Rime Relay	M	139
Fluency With Phrases			
• Increasing accuracy and speed in reading phrases	• Fast Phrases	M	144
	• Froggy Phrase Slide	M	145
• Reading with meaningful phrasing	• Step to the Beat	M	146
Fluency With Connected Text			
• Attending to punctuation cues in the text	• Say That Again	M	
• Reading with intonation and expression, using rhythm, feeling, voice, body movement	• Say It With Feeling	M	
	• Get the Beat	M	
• Increasing accuracy and expression	• Comics and Riddles	M	153
	• Tic-Tac-Poems	M	154
	• Class Favorites	M	156
	• Five Picks for Partner Reading	M	157
	• Write and Read	M	157
	• Buddy Reading	M	158
	• You Choose	M	158
	• Boomerang Reading	M	159
	• Read-a-Round	M	159
• Locating familiar words and spelling elements	• Find a Word	M	155
	• Highlights	M	155
	• Build a Poem	M	155
• Innovating on familiar text	• Change a Poem	M	156
• Visualizing (mental imagery)	• Movie in My Mind	M	154
• Monitoring for meaning	• The Big Picture	M	156
• Reading with increased speed	• Timed Reading	I, A	159
• Self-monitoring for fluency	• Three Then Me	M	158
Fluency With Technology	• Tape-Assisted Reading	M	168
	• Computer-Assisted Reading	M	168
• Using a modeled reading as a focus for repeated, independent readings	• Tell-a-Tape	M	169

Key: B = Beginner, I = Intermediate, A = Advanced, M = Multilevel

Assessing Word-Study Skills

The information gleaned from the phonics inventories and pseudo-word (or nonsense word) tests are important in guiding the specific spelling elements that students will use to build, read, and write words at the center. An example of a simple pseudo-word test is the Z-Test in McKenna & Stahl (2003), in which the letter *z* is used as the onset, resulting in words such as *zame* and *zate* to assess recognition of the rimes *-ame* and *-ate*. If you prefer to use real words, Patricia Cunningham's Names Test has been recently adapted (Mather, Sammons, & Schwartz, 2006) to provide a sequence of decodable "names" organized from easier to more challenging levels of word analysis. They also provide a separate Early Names Test with names representing short-vowel patterns, such as in the name "Rob Hap."

Tests of high-frequency word recognition and spelling typically consist of lists of sight words in order of frequency of occurrence, such as those found in *The Reading Teacher's Book of Lists* (Fry & Kress, 2006) and *Assessment for Reading Instruction* (McKenna & Stahl, 2003). From these lists, the words with irregular spellings that cannot be completely decoded or spelled according to regular patterns, may be organized into short study lists consisting of two to four irregularly spelled sight words for students to practice intensively at the center using the visual, tactile, and kinesthetic procedures. Such words typically require multiple practice opportunities before students develop a complete visual memory and are able to discriminate and record their unique letter sequence.

To assist you in planning for the word study center, resources such as *Words Their Way* by Donald Bear et al. (2004) and *Word Journeys: Assessment-Guided Phonics, Spelling, and Vocabulary Instruction* by Kathy Ganske (2000) provide a developmental sequence of instruction based on five spelling stages together with extensive word lists correlated to each stage (Emergent, Letter Name, Within-Word Pattern, Syllable Juncture, Derivational Constancy). Ganske's assessment, the Developmental Spelling Analysis, provides a teacher-friendly method to identify each student's stage of development through a whole-group dictation and analysis of individual spellings. The results may be recorded on forms organized by developmental level and specific spelling features, to be used as a guide for small-group instruction and center practice.

The Determining the Level of Challenge form (below) is designed to help you gauge the appropriate level of center activity for students, based on the decodable units and high-frequency words students are ready to read and spell. The Aligning Student Need chart (pages 30–31) lists the goals for word-study instruction alongside the activities that provide student practice. As you observe students write and construct words, you will be able to determine which of the areas of word-study practice are a priority for your students at this time, and list the corresponding activities on the center planning chart.

Determining the Level of Challenge: Word Study Center			
Skill/Strategy	**Beginner Level**	**Intermediate Level**	**Advanced Level**
Alphabet Recognition and Letter-Sound Relationships	Letter formation Upper or lowercase match (*B/b* or *E/e*) Initial or Final consonant (*me, can; hop, jam*) Medial Vowels (*cat, hen, dog, pig, bug*)	Initial consonant blends (*slip, frog, stop*) Two-letter initial consonant digraphs (*ship, chat, thin, when*) Two-Letter final consonant blends and digraphs (*last, bank; cash, rich*)	Three-letter initial consonant blends and complex consonants (*scream, throw, quick*)
Vowel Patterns	Short Vowel Patterns (*-at, -et, -ot, -it, -ut*)	VCe vowels (*lake, dime, bone*) Other common long vowels patterns (*day, light, hold, true*)	R-Controlled vowels (*far, her, fir, for, fur*) Abstract vowels (*toy, book, town*) Polysyllabic words containing common patterns
Compounds and Affixes	Two-syllable compound words (*something, anyone, basketball*) Suffixes (no change) (*-ed, -ing, -s, -es, -y, -ful*)	Three-syllable compound words Suffixes: consonant doubling (*plan/planning*) Suffixes: e-drop (*smile/smiling*) Prefixes (*unlike, misread, reread*)	Prefixes, Suffixes and other Syllable Patterns in Polysyllabic Words
High-Frequency Words	Shorter, more regular words; some with concrete associations (*my, we, his, on, and*)	Words with regular initial and final letter cues; same/different final letters, medial vowels; single consonant vs. blend or digraph (*said; them/then; want/went; were/where*)	Longer words with silent consonants, silent vowels, same sound—two spellings (*people; laugh; their/there*)

Aligning Student Need and Center Activities: Word Study Center

WHEN the student requires practice in	THEN provide these literacy center activities	Level of Challenge	Page Number
Alphabet Recognition and Letter-Sound Relationships			
• Printing letters using correct formation	• Tic-Tac-ABC Game • Letter Windows	B B	178 179
• Matching upper and lower case letters)	• ABC Flip Up	B	179
• Making the connection between letters and the sounds they represent and assigning the correct pronunciation	• Picture Sorts • Picture Flip Up • ABC Roll-and-Stack	B B B	179 181 181
• Using initial letter cues to generate words	• ABC Pick Up: Single Consonants • ABC Pick Up: Two-Letter Initial Blends & Digraphs • ABC Pick Up: Three-Letter Blends	B I A	181 184 185
• Comparing and contrasting words using initial, medial, and final letter cues	• Word Sorts: Initial, Final & Medial Letter Cues	B	182
• Comparing and contrasting two and three letter consonant clusters (blends and digraphs)	• Word Sorts: Initial Two-Letter Blends & Digraphs • Word Sorts: Three-Letter Blends	I A	184 185
Vowel Patterns			
• Recognizing familiar rimes within words	• Wrapper Rimes • Find-a-Rime • Word Games	M M M	188 190 191
• Generating new words by changing the onset or rime	• Magic Mat	M	187
• Comparing and contrasting words according to their rimes, other vowel patterns, or meaning associations	• Cut and Sort • What's the Same?	M A	189 195
• Generating and recording words using a specified rime	• House of Rimes • Flap Book	B B	192 193
• Using rimes they know to write a story or poem	• Story Rimes	M	189
• Building multisyllabic words using familiar rimes	• Build Big Words • Big Word Puzzles	I I	193 194
• Applying what they know to a menu of multisensory activities	• Tic-Tac-Rime #1, #2	B, I, A	193,195

Key: B = Beginner, I = Intermediate, A = Advanced, M = Multilevel

Aligning Student Need and Center Activities: Word Study Center

WHEN the student requires practice in	THEN provide these literacy center activities	Level of Challenge	Page Number
High Frequency Words with Irregular Spellings			
• Reading with accuracy	• Flip-Up Sight Words	M	206
	• Tic-Tac-Look-and-Say #1, #2	B, I, A	207
	• Sound Alikes (homophones)	A	209
• Using manipulatives to represent the correct letter sequence	• Mix and Fix	M	205
• Recording accurately	• Word Windows	B	206
	• Partner Tic-Tac-Read	M	206
	• Word Pyramids	I, A	207
• Comparing and contrasting words based on their letter sequence	• Sight-Word Sorts #1, #2, #3	B, I, A	207, 209
• Locating within text	• Sight-Word Hunt	M	206
• Constructing complete sentences	• Rebus Sentence	B	207
Compounds and Affixes			
• Building compound words	• Add-a-Word	B	214
• Recognizing familiar words within compound words	• Compound Flip Up	B	214
• Adding affixes to build new words	• Suffix Flip Up	I	214
	• Prefix Flip Up	I	215
• Substituting suffixes / prefixes to form new words	• Beginnings and Endings	A	215
	• Prefix and Suffix Flip Book	A	216

Key: B = Beginner, I = Intermediate, A = Advanced, M = Multilevel

Providing an Appropriate Level of Support

Once you've determined students' levels of challenge for each center and planned appropriate activities, you'll need to consider the level of support students need to accomplish the tasks. In this section, we'll examine several factors you can adjust to provide the support necessary for students to work successfully at centers. Keep in mind that not all students will require these supports in their learning environment to successfully complete their center tasks.

During small-group instruction, students practice strategy-based responses to their reading.

Teacher Support

Because DLCs are designed to support and extend the skills and strategies taught in small groups, they are an integral part of the cycle of teacher modeling, guided practice, and independent application (see Cycle of Support, page 48). If you notice that students are having difficulty with center tasks, review and reteach the skills and strategies (including learning strategies) in the small-group setting before students return to work independently on those skills in centers. Incorporate practice of common center tasks, such as word building and sorting, reading aloud fluently, and completing graphic organizers, into your small-group instruction to ensure that students can successfully complete this type of work independently.

Regularly scheduled student-teacher conferences are an important opportunity to ensure that every student understands both the skills and expectations of center activities. During this time, you can review center folders together and prompt students to share which activity they especially enjoyed, select what they consider to be their best work, and verbalize the thinking that led to this success.

Tap another source of information to guide your instruction and center planning: have students reflect on their work and identify one area in which they are experiencing difficulty or find "more challenging or tricky." This information, together with assessment data, can then be used to establish learning goals with the student, which will be referred to at the next scheduled conference.

Name _Brittney_ Date _September 24_	Reading Goals: • Use familiar vowel patterns to decode new words • Increase reading rate • Retell key events of a story in sequence
Observation/Assessment	**Instruction**
• Inconsistent use of phonics knowledge • Slow rate of reading • Retelling may not include all key events or be in sequential order	• Read words in lists, then connected text; prompt for visual cues during reading; center rime activities • Repeated reading in partner and group contexts; tape-assisted reading at center • Story structure visuals; pause and 'pair-share' during shared reading; short text and picture-cued cards at center

Allowing students to see the tracking mechanism you have in place (the recording sheet in your assessment notebook where you note needs and strengths by area of instruction) and a time designated for them on a calendar of student conferences, establishes accountability and helps them gain insight into their own learning process.

Peer Support

Much of what we know (adults included) is the result of experiences we've shared with others. Peer interaction is essential in DLCs, too. Cooperative tasks, such as partner reading, and game-like formats that you'll find in the center activities in Chapters 4–6 increase students' motivation and engagement while providing a supportive context for learning. Through the discussion that takes place during these collaborative activities, students clarify new concepts, and the skills they are practicing become concrete. Verbalizing the steps in completing a task also helps students internalize the skills and strategies

Peer support and feedback increase student engagement.

to be learned and set clear learning goals. Finally, as students build upon one another's understanding and ideas, their rate of skill acquisition increases, as do the depth and complexity of their oral, pictorial, and written responses to the task.

Learning Materials

Each of the literacy centers includes suggestions for learning materials that support students who experience difficulty with a particular skill or strategy. Some of these materials include leveled reading materials, books on tape, and concrete manipulatives such as magnetic letters, word cards, programmed cubes, and game formats. These are noted along with the activities in the chapter for each of the three centers.

Time and Pacing

Clearly, no classroom of students completes the same task in the same amount of time, whether it is a follow-up to a whole-class lesson or a center activity. This is one of the challenges we need to address within the center program. When you've begun your center work, one of the first factors to examine is whether the level of challenge is too difficult or too easy for a group or an individual student. If the activity is too challenging, there will always be the problem of providing catch-up time for incomplete work. If the activity is too easy, the student may become disengaged, and off-task behavior is likely to follow, along with the wasted learning time that results from lack of sufficient challenge. If students are working within their instructional zone, then they should be able to complete a task that is sufficiently challenging within the time allocated, without the problems of incomplete work. In Chapter 3, you will see how a Choice Menu is used to ensure that students who are truly "done" have tasks to engage them . . . and how incomplete work is tracked.

Teacher observation and assessment inform the pacing of our teaching and literacy program.

It is important to keep in mind that just because a student may take longer to complete an assignment, this does not mean that he or she is not putting forth a good effort; the child may process text at a slower rate or may require more time to record information because of slower-developing fine-motor skills. Many other factors (including those in the learning environment) may also impact a child's ability to complete a task within a given time frame. Teacher observation and assessment records are both important means to inform the pacing of our teaching and the time, text, and tasks we provide at the centers (Allington, 2005).

Practical options for addressing differences in our students' timing and pacing include:

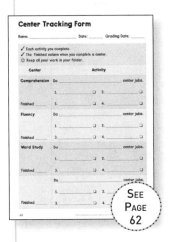

SEE PAGE 62

- keeping an individualized tracking sheet (see Center Tracking Form, page 62) with the number and level of activities to be completed at each center, clearly specified for each student (a number he or she can realistically achieve, within the time frame).

- adjusting the amount of text students read at the center and/or the recording requirements.

- having partners or small groups collaborate on a task.

- providing additional time to complete work before or after centers (when possible).

- allowing a student the option to skip certain activities at that center in order to complete a more extensive response to one particular task.

- the use of a digital timer and the activity or list of activities to be completed during a specific time period. (You can find a number of student-friendly timers, which provide a countdown format—a visual target that helps the child to develop self-pacing strategies).

Activity Level and Movement

Even when there are designated physical spaces for each center, you'll want to allow students to move around within these spaces, and you should consider this in the planning process. Students who require increased levels of movement and frequent breaks may be accommodated by a choice of standing rather than sitting to complete some of the assignments or by activities requiring kinesthetic learning (such as sorting word cards) that you incorporate in the activity choices for each center.

Physical Space and Noise Level

You may have students who work best in a quiet space of their own. For reading and writing tasks, allow them to work in an alternative space on the rug or around the perimeter of the room

Tip

A comfortable, relaxing space to curl up with a book encourages sustained reading.

with a clipboard in place of a desk or table. Or you may wish to provide the option of using a "student office" that includes a desk with a privacy screen made from a cardboard project display board. Equip the student office with writing tools and learning aids, such as the alphabet and word charts.

All students benefit from a comfortable area that encourages sustained reading. Soft cushions and stuffed animals (which can also serve as an audience) enhance the reading environment. Consider softer lighting where possible to avoid the problem of glare on white paper, and to enhance the quiet atmosphere.

Another option is to designate two or more areas for different noise level expectations (for example, a "no walking/no talking" zone for independent tasks not requiring movement and a "pair share" zone for interactive partner activities). Have students create picture-cued posters depicting the center activities for each zone, or use photos you have taken of students at work.

The Element of Choice

Each of us has our personal preferences for how, when, and with whom we work. There are some tasks we look forward to, and others we do not. Our students are no different. By planning to incorporate more than one activity at a center, we make choice for our students a possibility. Students may then decide which activity they will complete from the range of choices, or they may choose the order in which they complete the center tasks. It is important to note that all of the center activities the student may choose from in Chapter 4 are curriculum- and strategy-based literacy tasks; there are no poor choices to be made. The section Managing Literacy Centers (see pages 53–59 in Chapter 3) provides practical guidelines for incorporating choice while maintaining clear expectations and accountability at the same time. The decision to work independently or collaboratively can also be student directed. Different manipulatives for building words at the word study center and a wide range of reading materials at the reading comprehension center are examples of how the materials themselves provide for an element of choice.

In order to determine the type of support that will ensure success for each student, review the activities students will be working on at the centers, and consider the following: the demands placed upon them as readers and writers; how they will need to use the learning materials at the center; when, where, and with whom they will work; and how many activities you can reasonably expect them to complete. The Differentiated Levels of Support planning form can be used to record the needs and appropriate supports for specific students at each center.

Differentiated Levels of Support

Student	Centers	Support
Student: Devin	☑ Reading Comprehension ☐ Fluency ☐ Word Study	Time: • Activity Level: • Choices: See Tracking Sheet • Materials: clipboard • Partner: Courtney for reading support • Space/Noise: Student office • Movement:
Student: Selena	☑ Reading Comprehension ☑ Fluency ☑ Word Study	Time: • Activity Level: High • Choices: See Tracking Sheet • Materials: Manipulatives, timer • Partner: Kayla for Transitions Partner • Space/Noise: • Movement: Stand or sit
Student: Brittney	☑ Reading Comprehension ☑ Fluency ☑ Word Study	Time: • Activity Level: • Choices: See Tracking Sheet • Materials: Picture-cues, short structured- • Partner: James at Word Study • Space/Noise: • Movement:

SEE PAGE 38

Profile of the Learner

The third point of the Differentiated Learning Triangle is a profile of the student as a learner—his or her interests, attitudes, and strengths. We use this information to select and plan the center activities that will motivate and engage our students

Surveys of Student Interests and Attitude Toward Reading

Classroom observation, discussions, journal writing, open-ended questionnaires, interest inventories, and attitude surveys are all ways in which we can find out what motivates our students to extend themselves as readers and writers. Here are a few I recommend:

- The Elementary Reading Attitude Survey developed by Michael C. McKenna and Dennis J. Kear (1990), a five-page, picture-cued format including twenty questions, provides information on the student's attitude to both recreational and academic reading. The article containing this survey, "Measuring Attitude Toward Reading: A New Tool for Teachers," is freely available online from the International Reading Association archive of articles from *The Reading Teacher* at: www.reading.org or can be reproduced from the book *Assessment for Reading Instruction* (McKenna & Stahl 2003).

- Even more informal are simple "get-to-know-you" questionnaires and checklists like the one on page 39 which require students

"Student achievement is often a combination of intellectual ability and the ability to engage in learning . . . [Children's] ability to commit to a task and persevere can mean more than a history of high test scores."
(Drapeau, 2004)

Differentiated Levels of Support

Student	Centers	Support
Student:	❑ Reading Comprehension ❑ Fluency ❑ Word Study	Time: • Activity Level: • Choices: • Materials: • Partner: • Space/Noise: • Movement:
Student:	❑ Reading Comprehension ❑ Fluency ❑ Word Study	Time: • Activity Level: • Choices: • Materials: • Partner: • Space/Noise: • Movement:
Student:	❑ Reading Comprehension ❑ Fluency ❑ Word Study	Time: • Activity Level: • Choices: • Materials: • Partner: • Space/Noise: • Movement:
Student:	❑ Reading Comprehension ❑ Fluency ❑ Word Study	Time: • Activity Level: • Choices: • Materials: • Partner: • Space/Noise: • Movement:
Student:	❑ Reading Comprehension ❑ Fluency ❑ Word Study	Time: • Activity Level: • Choices: • Materials: • Partner: • Space/Noise: • Movement:

Differentiated Literacy Centers © 2007 by Margo Southall, Scholastic Teaching Resources page 38

to indicate the topics, book series, and authors they are most interested in reading. Students' responses can help you determine the reading materials for the comprehension center and classroom library. As students share favorite story characters, author series they enjoy, and topics they are knowledgeable about, they come to see themselves as readers, and this realization sustains their motivation on their journey to literacy.

- Send-home questionnaires for parents to complete can provide a profile of the child's interests and reading diet outside of school along with suggestions for making reading and writing a part of the child's daily routine.

- One-on-one conferences with students are an important tool for gleaning information about your students as readers and writers. The survey questions on page 40 provide a general guideline to determining students' attitudes toward reading at home and at school. Students are asked to list reading materials they enjoy, reflect on their areas of strength, and identify one skill or strategy they could acquire that would help them as readers. The responses to these questions provide us with information about the level of students' motivation and engagement, as well as their awareness of the reading process itself—what determines an effective reader and how this is reflected in their own strengths and areas of difficulty. The lack of self-confidence and subsequent low engagement levels commonly experienced by struggling readers requires the selection of high-interest-low-vocabulary reading materials for both the centers and instruction.

Reading Interest Survey	
My favorite topics to read about are:	**My favorite things to read are:**
❑ Animals (If so, what kind?)	❑ Poems
❑ Sports	❑ Mysteries
❑ Famous people	❑ Stories (Fantasy)
❑ Science topics	❑ Science fiction
❑ Real events	❑ Fairy tales
❑ How things work	❑ Magazines and comics
❑ Riddles and jokes	❑ Funny stories (humor)
❑ Adventure	❑ Series books (If so, which ones?)
❑ Other topics I like:	❑ Other types of texts:

Conference Questions:
Attitude Toward Reading Survey

Student: _____ Date: _____

- Do you like to read at school?

- How often do you read for enjoyment at home?

- Do you have a place where you like to read at home?

- What do you like to read?

- Do you have a favorite author? Series? Topic that you like to read about?

- What reading activities do you like best?

- What are you good at in reading?

- What are some areas that you would like to improve in?

- What do you need to do in order to become a better reader?

Differentiated Literacy Centers © 2007 by Margo Southall, Scholastic Teaching Resources page 40

Building on Student Strengths Using Multiple Pathways to Learning

Psychologist Howard Gardner's eight forms of human intelligence (1993) provide another frame in which to plan a differentiated center program—and you may wish to include the intelligences as an additional organizing principle for your centers.

As you examine samples of student work, consider the level of success students have experienced with the different processes the various tasks required. Were students more successful with some formats than others? These formats, organized by the eight intelligences, may include:

- Interaction with another student in a collaborative format, relating, interviewing (interpersonal)

- Manipulation of concrete materials, movement, dramatics (bodily-kinesthetic)

- Reading, writing, speaking, and listening (verbal-linguistic)

- Working alone on a self-paced project (intrapersonal)

- Creating images, drawing, mind-mapping, visualizing (visual-spatial)

- Using rhythm, song, patterned sound, rap, or dance (musical-rhythmic)

- Outdoor experiences; sorting, classifying, or patterning (naturalist)

- Working with numbers and patterns (logical-mathematical)

The multisensory formats incorporated into the center activities increase student success and engagement.

By providing tasks that reflect a selection of product forms, we are able to take advantage of the many types of intelligence present in our classroom. The chart on page 42 shows how some of the center activities included in this book correlate to the eight forms of intelligence.

Correlating Multiple Intelligences and Literacy Centers

Multiple Intelligences	Comprehension	Fluency	Word Study
Verbal/Linguistic Use oral or written language effectively	• I Wonder • Partner Quiz Cards • Talk to Author • Book Tub Buddies • Summary Frames • Tic-Tac-Question #3 • Who or What Am I? • Sum It Up Cube • Roll and Respond Cube	• Fast Phrases • Say That Again • Say It With Feeling • Comics and Riddles • Change a Poem • Tell-a-Tape • Write and Read • The Big Picture	• Word Games • Tic-Tac-Rime #1 and #2 • Build Big Words • What's the Same? • House of Rimes • Rebus Sentence
Musical/Rhythmic Perceive and communicate musically	• Reading Collections: songs, charts, raps, rhymes • Book Tub Buddies	• Partner Reading, Poetry • Get the Beat • Step to the Beat • Readers Theater—rap and rhyme scripts • Tape-Assisted Reading • Computer-Assisted Reading	• Story Rimes (Write poems, songs and raps) • Sound Alikes (homophones) • Word Play Book Tub Buddies
Visual/Spatial See the world through a spatial lens	• What Do I See, What Do I Know? • I See, I Wonder • Stop, Draw, and Write • Pyramid Summary • Picture Question Cards • Read, Relate, Respond • Connection Stems • Tic-Tac-Tell • Retelling Flap Book	• Step to the Beat • Get the Beat • Froggy Phrase Slide • Comparing Poems (Venn) • Highlights • Find a Word • Movie in My Mind • Class Favorites	• Picture, Letter, Rime, and Word Sorts • Wrapper Rimes • Flap Book • Find a Rime • Build Big Words • Big Word Puzzles • Prefix and Suffix Flip Book • Word Pyramids • Rebus Sentence
Logical/Mathematical Use numbers and reasoning effectively	• Facts and Questions • What's More Important? • Critic's Cube	• Fast Phrases • Partner Rime Relay • Timed Reading	• Picture, Letter, Rime, and Word Sorts • Word Pyramids • Roll, Read and Write • Flip Up (compounds, affixes)
Bodily/Kinesthetic Use body to perceive and express ideas	• Tic-Tac-Connect • Retelling Cube for Facts and Stories • Sticky Questions • Roll and Respond • Retelling Flap Book	• Word Reading Relay • Partner Rime Relay • Froggy Phrase Slide • Get the Beat • Build a Poem	• Magic Mat • ABC Pick Up Rimes; Roll a Rime • Picture, Letter, Rime, and Word Sorts • Add-a-Word • Flip Ups (Picture, Compound, Suffix, Prefix) • Big Word Puzzles • Build Big Words • Mix and Fix • Beginnings and Endings
Naturalist Comprehend the natural world	• Nonfiction Reading Collection • Tic-Tac-Tell for Facts • Who or What Am I?	• Nonfiction Poetry and Songs • Technology-Assisted Reading (nonfiction)	• Cut and Sort (open variation with nonfiction vocabulary)
Interpersonal Communicate with and understand others	• Character Close Up • Talk to the Author • Star Review • Partner Quiz Cards • Tic-Tac-Tell • Book Tub Buddies • What Kind of Questions Do They Ask?	• Five Picks for Partner Reading • Buddy Reading • Read-a-Round • Partner Talk • Three Then Me • Boomerang Reading • Readers' Theatre	• Tic-Tac-ABC Game • Partner Word Sort • Word Hunt • Rime Flip Up • Roll-a-Rime • Tic-Tac-Rime • Word Play Book Tub Buddies
Intrapersonal Assess one's own feelings, thinking	• Build a Connection • What I Think • In the Driver's Seat • Read, Relate, Respond • Critic's Cube • Connection Stems	• Say It With Feeling • Fluency Feedback Form • Movie in My Mind • The Big Picture	• Cut and Sort (open variation) • What's the Same? • Word Play Books

Differentiated Literacy Centers © 2007 by Margo Southall, Scholastic Teaching Resources page 42

From my own teaching experience and in my work with teachers across the country in professional learning contexts, I know that time constraints are a continual challenge as teachers juggle the instructional requirements of state, district, school, and students within their daily program. Unfortunately, this can lead to a dangerous "getting students through the program" approach to literacy instruction that neglects to vary the pacing and type of instruction. The result of such an approach is that many students do not receive sufficient practice to take a skill beyond short-lived rote recall to the level of mastery and understanding.

We need to maximize the precious teaching/learning time we have. This means identifying which activities will provide the most productive practice for our students at the centers—the process we've explored in this chapter. By analyzing the three sources of information represented in the Differentiated Literacy Triangle, we can determine which activities students are ready for and that will move them along the developmental continuum in reading, spelling, and writing.

In the next chapter, we will examine the how-to's of implementing DLCs in your classroom: the organization of students into groups, the rotation of groups through the centers, the number of activities they will complete, and the tracking of these activities to ensure that student accountability is built into our center program.

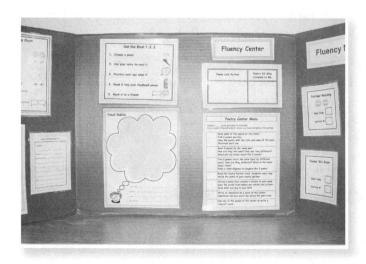

Center task cards attached to a project board display a set of activities students will work on throughout the year.

CHAPTER 3

Organizing and Managing Differentiated Literacy Centers

Not only are differentiated literacy centers a great way to differentiate instruction, they are also an effective management tool for keeping children actively engaged in purposeful learning while you meet with small groups. In my classroom I use DLCs while I meet with flexible reading groups to provide explicit instruction with leveled texts in comprehension, fluency, and word-solving strategies. This system allows me to go beyond whole-class teaching to provide more intensive instruction within needs-based small groups, while the rest of the class continues to develop literacy skills.

Maximizing this learning time requires efficient organization and thoughtful management of the centers in order to ensure that they run smoothly and productively. This chapter will show you how to get DLCs up and running and how to maintain them throughout the year.

Differentiated Small-Group Reading Instruction

Differentiated Literacy Centers Needs-based practice	Small-Group Follow-Up Needs-based reteaching/extension

Organizing the Physical Environment

You'll find reproducible center labels on page 57.

The three core centers do not each require a separate table or seating area in the classroom. I have successfully used these centers in classrooms where there was minimal available space. What makes it work are easily accessible activity materials labeled by center. Let's examine a few possibilities to help you make it workable in your classroom.

Permanent or Portable?

The perimeter of the classroom can be used to display and store center materials—on tables, bookcases, shelves, or bulletin boards, or in stacking units of containers.

File cabinets can become a magnetic word-building center and pocket charts can be hung on the door or back of a bookcase.

Existing clusters of student desks or tables can become a center. Identify these with a portable sign using the center icons provided on page 57, a flag (a pennant that is fastened inside a can with modeling clay) or table mat that can be stored on perimeter shelving during the rest of the day.

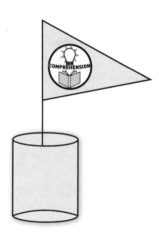

Students can collect the materials from labeled storage stations and take them to the center. You can also simply have students take the materials they need to their regular desks as a "carry and complete" activity.

Peace and Tranquility Versus Discuss and Discover

Location: Each center places different demands on the way students interact with each other and the materials. Students need a space that is conducive to the specific work designed for that center activity. The partner word-sorting activities at the word study center require verbal interaction, while a writing response activity at the comprehension center may be a quiet, independent activity. The center activities where student talking is essential need to be grouped together to support interaction, and located in an area that will minimize the distraction for students who are working on independent reading and writing tasks.

- The location of teacher-led small-group instruction during this time also needs to be considered in relation to these areas of individual work. Place your table where you can easily survey the rest of the class, while not disturbing or being disturbed by center interaction.

- Providing a designated quiet space where students can use clipboards for their writing and specially designated "reading chairs" (bean bag chairs) for independent reading helps to address the need for individual work space.

A word study center is set up with clearly defined work areas.

- When students are required to complete their activities at a table, you can establish clear boundaries for individual work space by setting a plastic table mat in front of each student or using masking tape to clearly mark four quadrants, one for each student at a table. This helps avoid issues of territoriality and respects many students' need for "their own space" within a larger community of learners.

Planning: To help plan your centers, complete a chart such as the one below. Use it as a guide to the location of specific center activities and the storage of the supporting materials.

Center Activity	Independent or Interactive	Location and Seating	Materials
Read, Relate Respond (C1 Multilevel)	Independent	Comp. Center table / low storage bins	• Cube • Reproducible

Traffic Zones: Students will need to move to collect and return materials, use technology, and come together for collaborative tasks. To avoid unnecessary interruptions to others and maintain a sustained focus on center work, designate traffic zones that minimize interruptions and maximize efficiency in student movement. As in a well-planned kitchen, there should be a triangular pathway to and from center materials and resources.

Store and Deliver, Retrieve and Recycle

We teachers are remarkably resourceful and organized individuals. Think of all the learning materials and papers that find their way to the students and back again each day in your classroom! The center resources found in this book and the hands-on learning materials and literature that support them require a manageable teacher- and student-friendly system for storage and retrieval. There are many excellent storage options for sale at business supply stores, container stores, and teacher resource stores. Some of these include:

- Small stackable tubs for storing cubes, game boards and dice, and other manipulatives

- Drop files or cardboard magazine holders labeled for each center, for filing center menu and activity task cards

- Twin pocket folders for keeping reproducible forms organized. (Glue a copy of the form to the outside of the folder to serve as a label.)

You'll find ideas for preparing center materials and activities on pages 59–67. Suggestions for organizing and displaying the specific materials for each center are described in the sections devoted to the three centers (Chapters 4 through 6).

Introducing the Center Activities

A cardinal rule for centers is that every activity you offer must be taught and modeled before students are asked to complete them independently. You can minimize the loss of precious teaching time by continually modeling and practicing the basic tasks and routines during ongoing whole-class and small-group instruction. For example, incorporating word sorting and partner reading into whole-class instruction helps students perform these tasks independently during center time.

This repetition of modeling and practice not only saves time but also addresses one of the key findings of the National Reading Panel and other researchers: students need increased opportunities for teacher modeling and independent practice, as well as more feedback, both from teachers and peers. One of the strengths of differentiated literacy centers is that they provide students repeated opportunities to apply new skills and strategies across multiple literacy contexts, which is critical if we are to ensure the transfer of classroom teaching to independent student application.

Cycle of Support

The process I use to introduce and reinforce center activities is known as the Cycle of Support (Pearson & Gallagher, 1983). This cycle consists of the following five steps:

Tell Me

First, explain and discuss how the skill and strategy incorporated in the center activity will help us grow as readers and writers. Connect it to whole-class and small-group ongoing instruction

Show Me

Then model how to apply the particular skill or strategy to the center task, making expectations clear. Next, ask a pair of students to complete the center task in front of their peers. Invite questions and articulate what you observe as the students complete the activity. Record this on a two-column Looks Like/Sounds Like chart to provide students with a visual and auditory model of how to do the work (see the word sort example below). These cues make your expectations for the center work explicit.

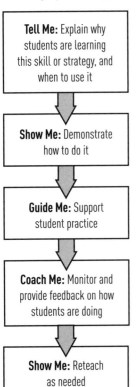

Five-Step Cycle of Support

Tell Me: Explain why students are learning this skill or strategy, and when to use it

Show Me: Demonstrate how to do it

Guide Me: Support student practice

Coach Me: Monitor and provide feedback on how students are doing

Show Me: Reteach as needed

Word Study Center: Word Sort Activity	
Looks Like	**Sounds like**
• Looking at the words • Sorting word cards on the mats • Writing words • Putting word cards back in the baggies	• Partners reading words to each other and saying what is the same about them • Silent writing

Guide Me

After the teacher and peer modeling, invite students to practice the task as a class or small group. For example, the graphic organizers, student picture-cue cards, and prompts in the comprehension center may be completed by students working together as a follow-up to a shared reading. Once most students seem confident performing a task, move the activity into the center for independent practice.

Coach Me

Monitor students' work in centers, offering feedback and planning to reteach as necessary. Take time to move around the room and observe student behaviors at the centers, even if it's only for five minutes between

Teachers incorporate the modeling and practice of strategy-based center activities into their whole-class instruction

reading groups. Note any behaviors or issues that need to be addressed. A daily debriefing is crucial. After each literacy center block, ask the following debriefing questions to the class as a whole:

- "What went well today?"
- "What needs to be improved? What could I/we do to prevent this from happening again?"

Help students brainstorm possible solutions to develop cooperative and independent learning strategies. You may need to add to or change the Looks Like/Sounds Like chart to take their suggestions into account. At this time, you can also raise any issues you noticed during your observations. Provide time for students to share their work and ask the daily review question:

- "What did we learn today to help us become better readers and writers?"

The centers are planned to reflect ongoing literacy instruction in whole- and small-group contexts. They reinforce and extend what has already been taught. By incorporating the same procedures in the center activities that you have demonstrated during the teacher modeling and guided practice steps in your lessons, you will not only maximize this precious literacy center learning time, but also make the expectation of independence an achievable goal.

Organizing Students Into Literacy Center Teams

Organizing students properly is key to the success of your centers. In this section, you'll find answers to key logistical questions about structuring the centers and grouping students.

How Many Centers Do I Need?

The number of students in your class and the number you wish to have at each center will determine whether you have all three centers up and running at the same time as well as three center teams. If you have all three operating continuously with sufficient activities for the whole class, you'll be able to use center time flexibly to administer assessments and confer with students. In this way you are not part of the rotation or a "teacher center." If you are a part of the rotation or also use a technology and/or small-group follow-up station in addition to centers, then you may not need all three centers at the same time. (See Rotation Options, page 53.)

How Many Students Should I Place in a Center Team?

How many students you will have in each center team will depend on whether you have a physical location with limited seating or your students will take center work to their desks. The physical location will also determine the number of copies of activities that you provide at each center. Tasks that need to be completed independently will require that every student have access to the necessary materials, copies of the task cards, and recording forms. The two options for organizing center activities described below will determine how you group students and the range of differentiated activities that you provide at the centers.

Options for Grouping Students

You have two options for grouping students at centers—homogeneous or heterogeneous grouping. Here are some detailed grouping tips, along with the advantages and disadvantages of each approach.

To homogeneously group or to heterogeneously group, that is the question.

Option 1: Homogeneous Grouping

With homogenous grouping, we create center teams based on students' placement in a guided-reading or skill-based group. Typically center team members are reading text at a similar level of complexity. However, the composition of the center teams changes as students are continuously regrouped according to their needs. All students in the center team work on activities at the same level of challenge, such as beginner. Some teachers will use a center activity as a follow-up to their small-group instruction. For example, students will complete a questioning activity at the comprehension center or a high-frequency word activity at the word study center using the book they just read in their reading group. These books and activities are placed at the center in bins labeled by reading group or in students' book boxes.

Advantage: Homogeneous grouping keeps organization simple: You maintain the same groups for both small-group reading instruction and literacy centers. Students rotate in the same group through centers and the small-group meeting during the literacy block.

Disadvantage: This grouping format allows less flexibility in grouping individual students for behavior purposes and for peer support.

Example: A class of 22 students is organized so that four to six students meet in their reading group while the remaining students are assigned to the center. (Note: Each student listed in the table below is identified by a number.)

Example of Homogeneous Grouping: Center Team #1 at the Comprehension Center—Questioning		
Differentiated Levels at Centers	**Students in Same Reading Group & Center Team**	**Center Activities**
Intermediate (Yellow)	1, 6, 10, 15, 17	Roll Up a Question Tic-Tac-Question #2

Option 2: Heterogeneous Grouping

Alternatively, you can create work teams that are heterogeneous and flexible. This leads to two types of flexible grouping: literacy center teams and reading groups. Students leave their teams to participate in small-group instruction, then return to the centers. At the center, they complete the activity labeled for their skill level. In this way, the common focus is the skill or strategy, but the level of complexity varies. For example, all the students at the center may complete a retelling activity on their small-group reading text. It works well to maintain the same student grouping for three to four weeks when students collaborate well together; you do not need to change the grouping each time you begin a new rotation of centers.

Advantage: The advantage of heterogeneous grouping is the availability of peer support for struggling learners and more flexibility for you to group students for behavioral purposes.

Disadvantage: Students may not have completed their center tasks when they are pulled to their reading group. Interruptions to partner activities will occur when one partner leaves the center, so independent tasks will also need to be provided at the center. A second rotation through the centers works best with this type of grouping (see Avoiding Catch-Up Time, page 54).

Example: The same class is organized so that four to six students meet at a center, regardless of skill level. Five students are assigned to the comprehension center and have to complete different activities.

Example Heterogeneous Grouping: Center Team #1 at the Comprehension Center—Questioning		
Differentiated Levels	**Students in Center Team**	**Center Activity**
Beginner (Green)	4, 19	I See, I Wonder
Intermediate (Yellow)	1, 15	Sticky Questions
Advanced (Red)	11	Tic-Tac-Question #3

Note: Not all students will work at the same level of challenge at all three centers, as their level of knowledge and understanding in the different areas of literacy instruction will vary. For example, one student may demonstrate higher levels of achievement in phonics than in comprehension. In this case, the tasks children work on at the word study center may be intermediate and located in a yellow file folder, while at the comprehension center they work on the beginner, or green folder tasks.

Managing Literacy Centers

Let's examine the day-to-day management of the center program to ensure students know which tasks they should be completing and are held accountable for the work they produce. The information in this section will provide a guide to the implementation of an effective management system to support productive center work and uninterrupted small-group instruction.

Rotation Systems

With a rotation system, all students systematically move through the three centers in their center teams. This allows you to control when and where students work on a given day. Rotation of students also ensures that every student participates in all the centers for a specific length of time and helps you avoid being driven by a Monday-to-Friday center schedule. Some teachers schedule centers four days a week and use that time on the fifth day for an extended block of whole-class instruction, such as teaching comprehension strategies in a shared-reading context with a district-mandated reading series, writer's workshop, and/or differentiated word study instruction.

Follow-Up to Small Group Instruction: A Fourth Center

You may prefer to use small-group follow-up activities as a separate "fourth center," with students completing this work at their desks before moving on to a center. If you choose to have a follow-up activity as part of the rotation in this way, then plan for the same amount of time as the center rotation. I typically allow 25–30 minutes at a center, which means the small-group follow-up assignment would need to reflect this time period.

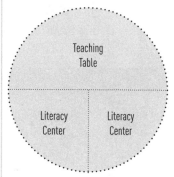

Rotation Options

Small-Group Instruction
+ 3 Centers

Small-Group Instruction
+ 2 Centers

Small-Group Instruction
+ Follow-Up Task + 2 Centers

Small-Group Follow-Up Task
+ 3 Centers

Avoiding Catch-Up Time

Your centers will operate most efficiently when you incorporate ways to support students who need to catch up as well as those who finish early. For instance, you may want to have students rotate twice through the same centers so that they have time to complete any work they did not finish in the first rotation. Having an opportunity to return to the same center menu of activities eliminates the need to schedule added time to complete unfinished work.

"I'm Done!": How to Keep Fast Finishers Engaged

You'll always want to plan activities that students may complete when they have finished the activities at their center. Having a set of "choice menu" activities allows students to leave their center when they have finished all the required tasks and select a new literacy-building activity. The choice menu can be displayed on the work board or on a separate poster or chart in the classroom. Activities may be based on current classroom themes, topics, or author studies and should be open-ended to accommodate the range of learners in your class. For example, students may: check out a book to read from the classroom library, read one of their independent leveled books from their book box, complete an activity related to a social studies or science theme or to an author study, free-write in their journal, or choose from commercially produced brain-based learning or literacy games.

Managing Center Rotation

I recommend using a visual tool, such as a rotation chart or wheel, to guide students to where they should be working. Keep in mind that the chart should be clearly visible from all areas of the classroom. For consistency and clarity, use the same center icons on the chart or wheel as you use to label center work spaces and containers for the materials (see page 57 for reproducible center icons).

Charts

One way to manage the rotation system is with rotation cards that show who goes where and are placed in a pocket chart or affixed to a magnetic or bulletin board. You will need two sets of cards, one showing the icons for the centers and another set with the names of the student teams.

How to Use the Rotation Charts

1. Prepare center icon cards and attach them to the rotation chart or place across the top or down the left side of the pocket chart.

2. Write the center teams on cards and place underneath or alongside the center icon cards. You may also rotate using pins, Velcro®, or magnets.

3. Rotate students through the centers by moving team cards in a rotation cycle; the center cards remain secured.

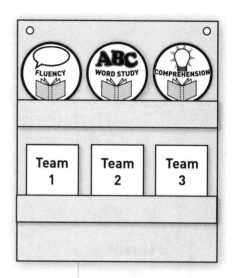

Wheels

Another way to manage the rotation system is with a rotation wheel.

How to Use the Rotation Wheel

1. Cut two circles from posterboard, one slightly larger than the other, and divide them into the same number of sections as there are centers. (So if you have three centers, divide each wheel into three sections.)

2. On the outer, larger circle, paste the center icons

3. On the inner, smaller circle, write the names of the center teams, or list numbers that represent individual students. If you laminate this circle you can fill in the names or numbers with a whiteboard marker so that they can be easily changed during the year.

4. Turn the inner circle to rotate the student teams to each center.

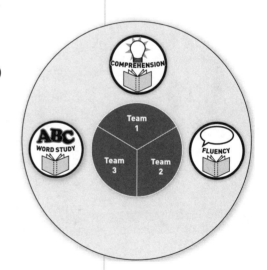

Student Behavior

Management issues concerning student behavior can arise as students move to a new center or have questions about an activity at the center. Establishing routines and having supports in place such as center monitors, can prevent problems from occurring. At the end of this chapter in the Quick Review section, you'll find a chart that provides a summary of the routines and formats that students need to be familiar with in order to work independently at the centers.

Supporting Transitions Between Centers

To support smooth transitions as students move between centers, review the routines and expectations each day before center time. Begin the year with a short time allotted for centers and gradually build up to your goal. For example, schedule only one small-group reading session during center time at first. Here are some tips for transition time:

- While students are learning the routines, gather them together during transition times to review what they are to do next.

- Alternate whole-class lessons and small-group/literacy center sessions to avoid long stretches of independent work time.

- Give a three-minute warning for students to finish up their activity and tidy up the materials. You may appoint a student "time tracker" to circulate with a sign as a reminder to their classmates.

- An overhead timer or traffic-light signal is useful for indicating transitions and can be used for each rotation period.

- Appoint a student "center checker" to ensure that materials are stored correctly and a "traffic director" to monitor and assist students as they rotate to their next center.

- Assign a transition partner to help students experiencing difficulty.

Routines to Support the 'No Interruptions' Rule:

When I reflect on behavior management during literacy centers, I am reminded of how I explained the self-help routines to my second-grade class after a summer trip to Surfer's Paradise, Australia. My mother is Australian (and responsible for my sense of humor) and had suggested this trip as a mother-daughter adventure. We were walking along the beach when we came across the shark attack sign recommending three things to do in case of a shark attack. (My comments follow each point.)

1. Remain calm. (I have every right to panic at this moment, thank you.)

2. Keep the affected part still. (Or ask the shark to kindly do so.)

3. Raise your hand for assistance. (Now this is taking politeness too far!)

As an elementary teacher, I saw a clear analogy between a shark attack and the routines of literacy center time. So, as I shared this

experience with my students, I transferred the advice from Surfer's Paradise to our classroom as follows:

1. Remain calm = Stop and think! If you can't find the pink highlighter or the flip book—breathe! Think of the options you have.

2. Keep the affected part still = Remain at the center!

3. Raise your hand for assistance = Please do not! Ask your team leader instead. If he or she is away or with me, then ask the team deputy (see below).

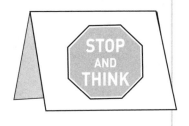

To avoid interruptions to small-group instruction you might display a "Stop and Think" sign or some other visual to indicate that this is a quiet time and students are expected to complete their work independently or in collaboration with each other. To help ensure that this happens, assign each literacy center team a leader and a deputy who will manage the materials, help maintain orderliness at the centers, and communicate directly with me as needed. These assignments should change for each new center rotation; if you have a weekly rotation through the centers, these positions will change weekly also. Center leaders and deputies may wear a clothespin or badge to identify their role to team members. If one of these students leaves the center to participate in small-group instruction, the other takes responsibility for answering any questions the team members have about the activities, as noted in the instructions above.

Establish the rule that only the leaders and deputies have access to you when the team encounters problems they cannot solve, such as students physically fighting. Other students may only interrupt the small-group session in the case of emergencies. My classroom emergencies include "blood, flood, and vomit," but you may add more to the list, such as visitors who arrive in the classroom unnoticed by you. Some teachers provide a designated spot for students to stand near the small-group reading table if they have an emergency or pressing need that requires teacher attention. Having students with behavioral difficulties work closer to you while you work with small groups may be necessary to provide additional supervision.

Keep in mind that when activities are too easy or too hard, problems often arise. To ensure that activities are not at students' frustration level, closely monitor student performance in that skill area and build on familiar reading activities, such as reading responses completed with the class. Tasks also need to be challenging enough to engage students and require that they apply previously taught skills and principles in novel ways.

The time allotted at each center can also affect issues of student behavior. Consider how much time you are allowing for center tasks. Is it too much or too little to time to complete a task? Plan 25–40 minutes at each center, depending on grade level and the number of activities you have provided for them to complete at that center. (Forty minutes will allow for two small-group lessons within one center rotation.) Nevertheless, it is important to be flexible. Some students may be doing an excellent job at one activity, and truly extending their own learning. Allow them to take additional time with this activity, perhaps take it to their seat to complete it and skip another activity at the center.

Back on Track Form

If a student is off-task and/or interrupting the learning of other students, you may require that he or she take the center work to a desk or a designated time-out area near the location for small-group instruction and fill out a Back on Track form. Provide this form in an easily accessible folder. Students write or draw a picture of what happened and how their behavior will change when they return to the center. Completing a Back on Track form provides an opportunity for students to redirect their thinking and actions in a positive way. Through regular review of the class expectations and the What should we see?/ What should we hear? chart, students will soon know which class policy they did not respect, and what they need to do now to get "back on track."

Assessing, Tracking, and Storing Student Work

Once centers are up and running, you'll want to monitor and assess student work so that you can plan new activities to keep students moving forward. This section provides guidelines for this process, assuring you get the information you need without getting overwhelmed by an avalanche of paper.

Store and Locate Activities Easily!
Center activities may be both color coded according to level of challenge and numbered for easy retrieval. For example, a beginner word sort comparing two short-vowel rimes at the word study center might be labeled "WS green, #7."

Center Tracking Form

Keep a center tracking form (page 62) in each student's center folder. When students have completed the activities at all the centers and samples have been selected for assessment purposes, the tracking form is used as a cover sheet and stapled to the completed reproducible forms. This booklet of center activities is then sent home and shared with parents.

Tracking Strategies

1. **Use the form as an individual contract:** The center tracking form can help students stay focused and organized as they move through the centers, selecting activities based on their individual needs.

2. **Track different levels:** To assist students working at different levels of challenge, be sure to clearly indicate the appropriate level for each center on their tracking form ("Center" column). Use your code to mark the level: color, letter, or other group designation. When levels are clear on the tracking form and on the materials at the centers, students quickly find the activities they need.

3. **Keep a detailed record:** Sometimes it is useful to fill in the full name of the center activity on students' tracking sheets so that you and parents have a clear record of what the child is working on.

Filling in the Form

- In the "Center" column, use the area under each center name to designate the appropriate challenge level for the student (student's level may vary at different centers).

- In the "Activity" column, record the number of activities you expect the student to complete. On the lines below, have the student write the name or number of the activities he or she has chosen (or pre-select and fill in the names of the activities). Then, as the student completes each one, he or she makes a check mark next to the activity.

- Initial and/or date the line marked "Finished" when the activities at the center have been completed.

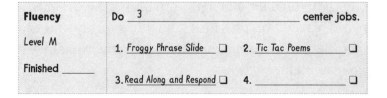

Fluency	Do __3__ center jobs.
Level M	1. _Froggy Phrase Slide_ ❏ 2. _Tic Tac Poems_ ❏
Finished _____	3. _Read Along and Respond_ ❏ 4. _____ ❏

I'm Back on Track

Name: _____ Date: _____

Off Track: What did I do?

On Track: What will I do now?

Name: _____ Date: _____

Off Track: What did I do?

On Track: What will I do now?

Differentiated Literacy Centers © 2007 by Margo Southall, Scholastic Teaching Resources page 61

Center Tracking Form

Name: _____ Date: _____ Grading Date: _____

✓ Each activity you complete.
✓ The Finished column when you complete a center.
☺ Keep all your work in your folder.

Center	Activity
Comprehension Finished _____	Do _____ center jobs. 1. _____ ☐ 2. _____ ☐ 3. _____ ☐ 4. _____ ☐
Fluency Finished _____	Do _____ center jobs. 1. _____ ☐ 2. _____ ☐ 3. _____ ☐ 4. _____ ☐
Word Study Finished _____	Do _____ center jobs. 1. _____ ☐ 2. _____ ☐ 3. _____ ☐ 4. _____ ☐
    Finished _____	Do _____ center jobs. 1. _____ ☐ 2. _____ ☐ 3. _____ ☐ 4. _____ ☐

Differentiated Literacy Centers © 2007 by Margo Southall, Scholastic Teaching Resources page 62

Balancing Teacher-Directed and Student-Directed Learning

If you are not using student tracking forms, you can balance teacher-directed and student-directed learning at the centers by designating must-do and may-do (or "you choose") center activities. The must-do activities can be indicated with a star or sticky flag on the folder or task card. In this approach, there are both must-do and may-do activities. You may designate a required number of may-do activities on the center rotation chart or at the center by placing a numbered sticky note or Velcro-backed number card on the center icon.

Choosing Products to Grade

First, consider how many grades you really need. When assessing student reading, only a sample is taken, perhaps with a running record. Apply this same rationale to center work and collect samples of student work at the each of the three core centers. Though I do not mark every student's page in detail, I do check them all briefly. I make a note on any student pages where the student has demonstrated difficulty, often bracketing the example of student work and initialing it, so parents know I am aware and addressing this area of need. A time-saving solution is to use two stamps on student work – one that says "Practice to Learn" or "Independent Practice" and another that says "Practice with Support" or "Guided Practice". These let students and parents see that students' work is being monitored. The stamps also mark the difference between teacher-managed activities and those the student has completed independently, without teacher support.

Share with students how their center work will be used to determine their grades during this reporting period. You may tell students that you will be selecting one sample from each of the three centers without telling them which activities they will be. By randomly selecting their work, you require that students put forth a good effort for all center activities. Alternatively, ask students to select what they consider to be their best work and ask them to add it to their portfolio or place it in the designated tray. Display a benchmark example of student work to reinforce expectations for work products at each center.

Not all centers will have a paper record. This is not a problem when samples have been collected from other centers, whole-class and small-group activities, and ongoing informal assessments.

Must do

Tracking and Storing Student Work

You have several options for tracking and storing student work. Whatever option you choose, you'll want to make sure that students assume responsibility for placing their work where you can easily retrieve and review it, so modeling the process you choose is essential. Several options are described below.

Center Folder: Provide each student with one twin-pocket folder to store the recording forms from all the centers. These pocket folders are stored in a bin. One pocket of the folder can be used to store a tracking sheet, checklist, or recording form, while incomplete work is placed in the other pocket to be completed first on the next rotation to that center when students are rotated twice through the same centers.

Another option is a four-pocket folder that enables teachers to direct unfinished or unsatisfactory work back to the student for completion or editing. A four-pocket folder can be quickly constructed by stapling two twin-pocket folders back to back. The four pockets are labeled as follows:

1. My Menu (list of center activities to be completed)

2. I Need to Finish (work the student will complete on the next rotation at this center if there are two rotations, or the first activity they will work on the next day)

3. I Need to Fix (work that requires completion or editing that the student has placed in the Take Home pocket)

4. I Am Finished (placed here by student, then checked by the teacher, who may move this back to pocket #3)

1.	2.	3.	4.
My Menu	I need to finish.	I need to fix.	I am finished.

Hanging File: This can provide a student filing system, with three dividers labeled with the three centers. Students file the recording sheets according to each center.

Hand-It-In Bin: Students place completed work in a tray or bin at each center, or you may provide a bin for each team to put their work in when they are finished.

Recording and Reviewing Progress

You may choose to use one small-group reading instruction period every two weeks or daily independent reading time to hold regular student conferences to review and discuss their center work. Give students a date on which you will meet with them. Create a chart displaying the class conference schedule for each two-week period or note the conference date on individual student tracking sheets to encourage ongoing review and self-monitoring (see Center Tracking Form, pages 60 and 62). By planning regular check-up times, both students and teachers are kept informed of any area of difficulty that may arise.

Another way to monitor center work is to offer small-group feedback. Have students bring their center folders with them to their reading/literacy group for a quick check and some feedback. Discuss areas of strength and need and use this collaborative context to congratulate students on their successes, both academic and creative.

With either system, you'll want to use samples of student work to identify teaching points and debrief/review topics.

Important Forms to Use and Formats to Follow

Reproducible Forms, Task Cards, and Notebooks

Reproducible forms are provided with many of the activities in Chapters 4 to 6. These forms can be stored and displayed in twin-pocket or file folders, that are labeled with a sticky dot or other coding system to indicate the level of challenge. Where possible, reduce photocopying by having students copy the format from a task card into their center notebook and then record their responses.

(Create a task card by pasting or copying the form on card stock and laminating it.) A two-column format can be easily replicated in a notebook by showing students how to fold their page to the center. You may prefer that students use a separate notebook for recording reading responses at the comprehension center and word study centers. Students' notebooks may be kept in their center folders.

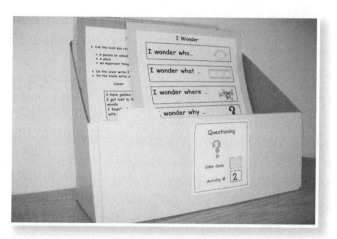

Menu cards are used to label a magazine holder containing task cards for the center activities.

Menu Cards

Picture-cued center menu cards representing the strategy or skill area are included at the end of each of the center chapters. For example, the comprehension center includes picture cards representing Making Connections and Self-Monitoring, Generating and Answering Questions, Retelling and Summarizing, and Evaluating. These can be photocopied and used to label containers and folders with center materials. There is a space on each card to note the challenge level and to write the activity number.

Tic-Tac-Toe Formats

This format is used at each of the centers and supports developmentally appropriate programming while allowing students to choose among two or more activities. It also incorporates multiple-intelligence principles. By selecting three options and responding in a gamelike format, students demonstrate a high level of engagement and success in these activities. The tic-tac-toe board is used as a menu for students to select from; in collaborative activities, the board accommodates individual student preferences and needs.

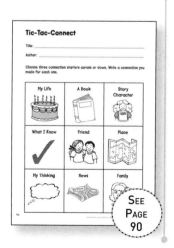

SEE PAGE 90

To create the tic-tac-toe board, paste or copy the reproducible form onto the appropriate color of card stock and laminate it for durability. Some teachers provide game markers or simple cutouts for students to place on the spaces of the chosen activities. Other options include cutting apart the nine squares into individual cards and displaying them in a 3- by 3-inch grid in a desk-top pocket chart or hole-punching the cards and clipping them together with an O-ring.

Cubes

A number of the activities at each level require the use of a cube. Cubes are used to incorporate a gamelike, kinesthetic element into the learning to engage young readers. Their instructional purpose is to provide variety in completing the skills-based tasks that you place on each side of the cube. To make a cube, use card stock to photocopy the cube reproducible included with the center activity directions. To clearly differentiate the three levels of cube activities, copy the leveled activities onto the corresponding color you've chosen for Beginner, Intermediate and Advanced (e.g., green, yellow, red) and attach to the sides of a 4- by 4-inch foam core or plastic cube. You can also cover cube-shaped tissue boxes or gift boxes designed for coffee mugs with paper and paste or tape the prompts onto each face.

There are several adaptable cubes available through teacher stores and catalogues that have clear pockets in which you can place prompt cards. When using these, copy the cube activity form onto the color of card stock for that level or paste the activity onto index cards and cut the cards into a 3- by 3-inch size. In this way the cubes may be quickly reprogrammed for different activities and levels of challenge. Cards can be stored in an index card holder with dividers for each center, and then organized by skill area and level of challenge (color).

The six activities on the cube form can also be used as a menu task card. Specify the number of activities you wish students to complete and allow them to choose these from the six possibilities. For partner activities, you may wish to cut apart the six cards and display on book rings or in resealable bags. Partners can then take turns using these as prompt cards.

A Quick Review for Success With DLCs

Many questions typically arise regarding the management of literacy centers. In this section you will find summary charts and a concise FAQ format to place the answers to these at your fingertips.

What Students Need to Know and Practice	
What Students Need to Know	**What to Model and Have Students Practice**
Where to work and what to do	• Reading the Management Board • Recognizing the tidy-up and transition signals • Moving from center to center • Reading the center menu cards • Identifying which activity to complete by checking their tracking sheet (color code, number, name of the activity)
How to work effectively in a group or with a partner	• Turn-taking, sharing materials • Asking for and giving help in an appropriate manner • Respecting the authority of team leaders and other center monitors • Participating in partner formats (e.g., partner word sorts) • Participating in group formats (e.g., Boomerang Reading)
Completing center tasks	• Expectations for each center activity • What an appropriate response looks like using a student example or peer role-play
Using and storing center materials	• Using materials for each center activity • Returning materials to correct locations in a timely manner
Who to ask for help	• Performing the duties of team leaders and deputies • Seeking out class experts (e.g., who can help with spelling or computer) • Knowing how to solve the problem yourself and continue working on task • Following the "No Interruption" rule, except in emergencies • Recognizing what is an emergency and what is not, what to do if there is an emergency
What to do when "I'm done"	• Selecting from the choice menu
Where and how to store their work	• Using the student pocket folder to store unfinished and finished work or placing it in the designated spot at the center

FAQs

Do I need to individualize all of my center activities?

Differentiated instruction is not synonymous with an individualized program. Rather, groups of students within any one classroom demonstrate similar profiles of needs and interests. By focusing on groups of students the teacher is able to establish a manageable, sustainable number of center activities that address the profiles within their classroom (see Organizing Students Into Literacy Center Teams, page 50). Multilevel activities are also included for each center.

How many centers do I need?

The answer to this question depends on a number of factors: whether a physical location is being used for each center, which limits the number of children who may work there; the number of students in the class; and the availability of multiple copies of center task cards and supporting materials (see Organizing Students Into Literacy Center Teams).

How many students should I have in each center team?

This will depend on whether there are designated physical locations for the centers with limited seating at each. If all of the three core centers you are implementing are transportable, with students taking work to their seats, then the number in each team is not as important. Typically there are three to six students in a literacy team. Keep in mind that not all activities require collaboration. Plan a balance of activities that are designed for collaborative and individual effort, especially when you have heterogeneous grouping and some students may leave that center to participate in small-group instruction. For example, the activities using cubes and tic-tac-toe formats lend themselves to team efforts, while many other activities are geared more toward individual completion (see Organizing Students Into Literacy Center Teams).

Should I allow students to choose their own centers or activities?

It's best to provide controlled choices within students' developmental "zones" along with open-ended activities at each center that allow opportunities for students to extend their learning and exercise their individual creativity. Choices are designated on a central planning board and/or student tracking sheets (see Rotation Systems, page 53).

How long should students remain at a center?

Typically students remain at the center for 20–35 minutes. Remember, there is always more than one activity to complete at each center. You may choose to take five minutes to supervise the transition between the centers. The number of rotations you have in a day will depend on the length of time scheduled for small-group instruction. Some classrooms have 30–40 minutes, and others have 90, which allows the teacher to work with multiple small literacy groups each day (see Student Behavior, page 55).

Do I need to have new centers each week?

The three core centers remain in place for the entire school year. It is the activities at each center that change. They change in terms of the level of challenge, formats, and materials. You may have students rotate twice through the activities, so that they may complete all the assigned tasks, including some open-ended activities that allow students to extend their learning. (Keep in mind that you'll also need to provide choices for students who have completed their assigned work.) The number of centers you need in a given time period will also depend on whether you have a small-group follow-up activity and/or a technology station in addition to centers (see Managing Literacy Centers, page 53).

What if they finish all their center work?

Every teacher dreads the two little words "I'm done" during literacy center time. The first way to avoid this is to select activities for students based on the appropriate level of challenge and consider the amount of reading and writing required to address individual differences. Ensuring that your students are working within their instructional zone will help to avoid the continual challenge of providing additional 'catch-up' time. Second, in any rotation or self-selection system there must be clear expectations about what students may do when they've completed all their center activities. For example, you might display a menu of choices on the center rotation chart. These may include thematic activities, class author studies, individual research projects, educational board games, or other activities that require little in terms of teacher preparation (see Choice Menu, page 54).

What if students rush to get to the computer-based activities?

Working on the computer is always a popular activity, so it should not be a choice activity, or some students may rush to finish their center work. Computer-based work activities should be part of a class rotation where each child's turn is protected. If a student is called to small-group instruction, then his or her name remains unchecked on the computer list and that student has priority in the turn-taking sequence. In some classrooms, students may place a name card on the computer to reserve it for when they return from small-group instruction. Technology options can also be integrated into the centers themselves, such as the Technology-Assisted Reading activities at the fluency center (see Chapter 5).

How can I ensure that students produce quality work at centers?

- Display samples of student work as clear examples of the level of work you expect.

- Allow students to participate in guided practice of center tasks and provide them with feedback.

- Select samples of each student's work for evaluation and teach to areas in which students need support in your ongoing instruction in the classroom.

- Continue to practice the routines and activities in whole- and small-group contexts, as well as provide opportunities for students to share their work on a daily basis (see Assessing, Tracking, and Storing Student Work, page 59).

How can I support the English language learners in my classroom?

Students whose native language is other than English will benefit from additional modeling, picture cues, and peer support. Background information and vocabulary building are long-term goals. Where possible, provide directions and reading materials in their own language and the opportunity to share their work with someone in their own language, such as a peer, older student, volunteer or parent.

Getting Started: Six Steps to Success

In the first three chapters we have examined all the important factors in planning, managing, tracking, and preparing the centers. The six steps below provide a summary of this information and serve as a "teacher checklist" for successfully implementing the differentiated literacy center activities in the following chapters.

Step 1 Assess the learners to determine performance levels and instructional zones.

Step 2 Observe individual students to determine the level of support they require at the center. This may include both access to peer support, as well as modifications in the learning environment, activity level, and types of learning materials.

Step 3 Provide a variety of tiered assignments that incorporate multisensory, multiple-intelligence learning opportunities to meet the needs of the diverse learners within each and every literacy center team.

Step 4 Decide upon the number of center teams and students within each team. Select and construct a management system and accompanying visual to guide center rotations.

Step 5 Plan and prepare center activities that directly support your instruction, based on the information in steps 1–3.

Step 6 Introduce and practice the center activities and rotation system in whole- and small-group contexts. Schedule time for continued modeling, problem-solving discussions, and student sharing.

Now that we have examined the instructional possibilities of differentiated literacy centers and have a management system in place for their implementation, we are ready to select activities for each of our centers and watch our students' literacy skills grow!

Have I . . .

❏ **Prepared activities with a reproducible page?**

Tip: Make enough copies for the number of students who will be working on this activity and store the copies in a labeled folder

❏ **Prepared activities with a reproducible template that students will copy in their notebooks?**

Tip 1: Make a task card by copying the reproducible onto card stock, laminating it, and displaying it at the center. (Note: Some notebook activities require students to make a two-column chart, which they can easily create by folding their notebook page in half to meet the binding and creasing the paper along the fold.)

Tip 2: Students may use dry-erase markers to write on and wipe off their answers on laminated task cards instead of writing in their notebooks.

Tip 3: Display task cards and any charts with student directions on a project display board or bulletin board. Attach with Velcro for quick changes as you change the activities during the year (see page 43).

❏ **Prepared activities with card sets?**

Tip: Make several copies of the reproducible page on card stock. Cut the cards apart and place each set in a small, resealable plastic bag. Alternatively, punch a hole in the top left corner of each card and clip them on an O-ring. Cards shaped as long, horizontal strips, such as sentence-starter prompts can be held together with a paper clip and stored in a jar.

❏ **Prepared activities with no reproducible page (notebook responses or talk-based work)?**

Tip: Make a task card or chart to model how to record the information or how to participate.

❏ **Labeled the center folders?**

Tip: In a separate folder, place copies of each reproducible page you'll feature at the center. Label the folder by gluing a copy of the reproducible to the front cover.

❏ **Labeled center workspace and containers of materials for each center?**

Tip: Use the center icons on page 57 to make center placemats or flags (see page 45), label containers of manipulatives and other materials students will require at the center.

❏ **Clearly marked leveled materials?**

Tip: Color code or otherwise mark the level of each activity on the folder or task card. This helps children quickly find the activities that they will be working on ("Your team is working on activities in the green folders") and helps you organize and store your materials efficiently. (See tips for color coding materials, page 59.)

Die Option for Card Sets

Provide a die with the numbers 1 through 6 and number each card. Students roll the die, select the card with that number, and follow the directions or use the prompt given.

CHAPTER 4

Differentiated Learning at the Comprehension Center

"Comprehension, or an understanding of the text varies with every reader. No two readers will produce exactly the same meaning from a text . . . How readers apply different strategies as they process text, however, will influence the depth of their understanding."
(Johns & Lenski, 2000)

We know that the amount of time spent reading connected text is directly correlated to reading achievement (Allington, 2005) and that struggling readers often spend less time than their on- or above-level peers reading and within instructional contexts that focus on comprehension (Johns & Lenski, 2000). A key instructional goal, then, is to make sure that we provide center activities that engage students in sustained reading of connected text with a strategic focus.

The comprehension center activities featured in this chapter are organized into four strategy-based areas, including

1. Making Connections and Self-Monitoring

2. Generating and Answering Questions

3. Retelling and Summarizing

4. Evaluating and Determining Importance

You'll find that these activities also incorporate research-recommended strategies such as inferring, visualizing, and synthesizing (McLaughlin, 2002; Cooper, Chard & Kiger, 2006).

How the Center Works

At the comprehension center, students engage in the following activities:

• selecting reading material labeled at their independent reading level.

• locating the supporting reading response they are to complete.

- reading the text.
- writing or drawing and labeling the responses they made to the reading material. This may be completed during or after the reading.

Note that reading response graphic organizers and picture-cued prompts are provided for many of the activities. Research has demonstrated how all students benefit from the use of graphic organizers (Flynt & Cooter, 2005) and the organizers provided are designed for students at all levels. For struggling students who find a blank piece of paper very intimidating, graphic organizers provide an appealing structure to help guide their responses. When we give students who are ready for a challenge an opportunity to respond within the supportive framework of an organizer, they often express their ideas in more expansive ways.

Teaching Tips for the Comprehension Center

1. **Model and Allow Time for Students to Practice:** The selection of your center activities will be based on your current focus in the area of comprehension instruction and on corresponding student assessment data (see Chapter 2). In order for students to complete the activities independently, first introduce the activities and practice them in a whole-class and/or small-group context (for a list of Resources see page 133).
   - Model the thinking processes required of the comprehension strategy by "thinking aloud" at each stopping point in a shared reading or read aloud.
   - Show students how to fill in the reproducible form for the activity you've chosen (use an enlarged version of the form or a copy of the form on the overhead). Or, if no reproducible is used, demonstrate how to respond to the reading by writing your response on chart paper or the overhead.
   - Have students practice independently and monitor for understanding. Reteach as necessary. Only when students can work on the activity unassisted should you place it at the center.

2. **Use Visual Aids:** Display the comprehension strategy charts and other graphic organizers that you have created together as a class in response to ongoing reading experiences, for students to use as a reference.

Strategy Lessons for the Whole Class
Teach each comprehension strategy to the whole class and introduce procedures for leveled activities to small groups. This way the class has a common focus and *multiple strategy-based lessons are not required.*

3. **Use Work Samples:** As you model and reteach, use examples of student work from the center and invite students to share their connections, questions, visual images, and retellings.
   - Compare the different connections and questions students generated about the same stories or topic.
   - Discuss how our different experiences result in a variety of connections and questions: "How did our connections or questions help us understand the story [or the information presented]? How did our questions help us grow as readers?"

4. **Display and Showcase a Reading Collection at the Comprehension Center:** A rich book selection that's leveled appropriately and arranged attractively will improve time spent reading and the quality of students' responses.
   - **Book Displays:** If students are selecting books during the center time, display the books for the center in tubs labeled by the reading level with the covers facing outward so they are easily accessible to students.
   - **Student Book Boxes:** To increase the amount of time students spend reading at the center and decrease the time they spend browsing for books, I provide individual student book boxes (introduced in Chapter 1) containing two to four books at the students' independent reading level. These are teacher-selected books that we have read during guided reading and self-selected books that students have chosen during a morning book exchange, one of our entry routines each day. If you build the book exchange into your routine, make sure it is monitored each week by several student librarians who check that books are placed back into the correct labeled bins and re-sort books as necessary.
   - **Multilevel Take-Out Tubs:** Maximize the potential of the books you have in your classroom to reach the right readers by sorting some of them into take-out tubs. Create mini-collections of reading material in bins or tubs with an icon that depicts the topic, theme, genre, or author.

Vary the tubs you display during different center rotations so that they relate to your instruction and students' interests. I find it helpful to use a copy of my curriculum calendar for the year to create a reference list of supporting comprehension center reading

Storing Book Boxes

Student book boxes can be stored in bins or bookshelves labeled in alphabetical order, at or near the comprehension center. I use cereal or taco boxes cut in half, or magazine holders, with the child's name printed on the shortest end, which faces outward for easy retrieval and maximizes storage space (see example, page 8). Some teachers use individual storage bags, like small backpacks, which can be hung on the back of student chairs. Another option, clear plastic book bags, available from teacher resource catalogues, can be hung on a rack or stored in bins labeled by literacy team or reading group.

materials. This enables me to select materials that will support the specific topic, skill, or strategy and add to these on an ongoing basis as I discover new ones.

5. **Give Students Opportunities to Respond to Their Reading With a Peer:** Encourage students to meet in pairs at a favorite tub (make sure to have available interest-based tubs with books at a variety of levels to support heterogeneous grouping). Tub buddies can discuss a title, author series they enjoy, or topic they are interested in researching (study buddies). This exchange enables students to deepen their understanding of the text by piggybacking off the thoughts of their peers, much as literature circles and book clubs do, but in a partner format that is manageable for younger students. This collaborative reading activity provides a motivating context for students to engage in reading and responding to text for sustained periods of time.

Activity formats in this chapter that help guide peer discussions include tic-tac-toe boards, cubes, and question cards. Tub buddies may take turns or collaboratively respond to the prompts. Once students are familiar with the type of reading responses, the recording options can be more open-ended. For example, students may keep a reading journal to record their personal responses to the reading. Partners can exchange journals, read and respond either orally or in writing.

Exchanging responses to the text with a Tub Buddy enables students to deepen their understanding of a common text.

Tub Buddy Activities

- Provide a selection of multilevel texts within each collection of tubs, including books with predictable, patterned text and easy chapter books, to allow participation by every student.

- When a reading series or topic catches the interest of students, take their lead and add to the center collection and book tubs. As you update materials in this center, take a few moments each week to highlight some of the new additions to encourage students to explore different genres throughout the year.

- Schedule time for brief book talks so that students can recommend titles they have recently read. Allowing three to five minutes a day of sharing their reading experiences with peers encourages students to increase their "reading mileage" and reach outside their comfort zone to try a more varied reading diet.

> "Proficient readers search for connections between what they know and the new information they encounter in the texts they read" (Pearson, 1992 in Harvey & Goudvis, 2000).

Making Connections/Self-Monitoring

Overview of Activities: Making Connections/Self-Monitoring				
Topic	**Activity**	**Level**	**Page**	**Repro**
Making Connections / Self Monitoring	• Read, Relate, Respond	M	79	84
	• What Do I See? What Do I Know?	B	80	85
	• Connection Stems	B	80	86
	• What I Think	I	81	87
	• In the Driver's Seat	I	82	88
	• Build a Connection	A	82	89
	• Tic-Tac-Connect	A	83	90

Teaching Tips

- Students who struggle to make connections to the text require a supportive structure to make all three levels of connections—to their life experiences, to other texts, and to events and issues in the world around them (Harvey & Goudvis, 2000). Advanced students require a framework for extending their connections to include responses that incorporate higher-level thinking. Readers have both intellectual and emotional connections as they read. Both are equally valid and each is supported within these differentiated reading comprehension activities.

  - **Text-to-Self Connections:** Encourage and model for students how to make connections that resonate with their lives and draw them closer to the text. Focus on events and ideas that reoccur across the text, rather than minor details such as individual words that are useful only on that one page (Miller, 2002).

  - **Text-to-Text Connections:** You may display a cumulative chart of books and other reading materials that you have read together as a class to support these connections. Introduce and make a list of the types of text-to-text connections students can make, such as comparing characters' personalities and actions, story events, themes or messages the author is trying to convey, and different versions of the same story.

  - **Text-to-World Connections:** Many of the stories we read aloud to students may reflect issues and events taking place in the world beyond the classroom. World issues and events are often reflected in nonfiction magazine articles students may read and discuss, and can also be found in literature where a character is in conflict with larger societal issues, such as the prejudice depicted in the books written on the life of Ruby Bridges. Historical fiction and nonfiction, biographies, and survival stories depicting conflict with nature often provide examples for this type of connection.

- Try to make available a selection of books with characters that students can identify with, perhaps in their own age range and/or from sociocultural contexts that they can relate to. Series books with consistent characters make excellent resources as students are able to build their understanding of how and why a familiar character responds to situations in a characteristic way.

Activities

Read, Relate, Respond

Purpose: Students will explore intellectual and emotional connections to their reading and monitor for understanding when events or information are puzzling or confusing.

Materials

- Read, Relate, Respond reproducible (page 84)
- folder or cube
- scissors and glue (cube option)
- student notebooks (notebook option)

Preparation

1. For individual response sheets, make copies of the reproducible and place them in a folder at the center. If students will respond in their notebooks, make several task cards by laminating copies of the reproducible.
2. For a cube format, copy the reproducible onto card stock, cut apart the six pictures, and attach them to the six sides of the cube (simple cube-making ideas are included on page 67).
3. Model each type of connection before assigning in the center.

Procedure

1. Students choose a type of connection from the reproducible or roll the cube.
2. Students use the picture cue and key word to write about a connection they've made to an independent reading book. They fill in the graphic organizer, recording their responses on the reproducible or in their notebooks.

Modeling Tips

1. Demonstrate by sharing your responses to an event or fact in a big book or a passage on the overhead projector. Read further and invite student responses.
2. Brainstorm with students a vocabulary chart of emotion words that they can use as a reference for this activity This will extend their thinking beyond a simple "sad / mad" response. Present hypothetical situations that would cause them to respond emotionally and ask them to show you with their faces how they would feel (for example, frightened, embarrassed, surprised, excited, amazed, worried, confused, angry, or happy). You may ask a student volunteer to illustrate the chart with facial expressions (see also the emotion cards on page 161).
3. Discuss how each picture cue represents a specific type of response during the reading

   - **I think:** Did students find a part that caused them to think more about the events or information?
   - **I feel:** Did students have an emotional response to events in the story or about the facts they just read?
   - **A funny part is:** Which parts made them laugh or smile?
   - **A surprising part is:** Did they find a surprising part in the reading?
   - **Wow! An exciting part is:** Did they discover an amazing fact or find a part that grabs their attention?
   - **This is puzzling:** Do they need clarification on something they've read? All readers need to use fix-up strategies as they read to problem-solve words, ideas, or facts that they find confusing. Model monitoring for understanding by reading and stopping at designated points in a read-aloud and verbalizing 'fix-up' strategies when comprehension is lost, such as:
     - ✓ reread the sentences before and after
     - ✓ use picture cues
     - ✓ look for familiar parts of words (letters, vowel patterns, root words, and affixes)

✓ think of another word that looks like this word

✓ think about what makes sense

Beginner Level

Activity 1

What Do I See? What Do I Know? (Visual Literacy)

Purpose: Students will connect prior knowledge and experience to the pictorial representation of characters, events, or information in a book.

Materials

- What do I see? What do I know? reproducible (page 85)
- folder or student notebooks

Preparation

1. For individual response sheets, make copies of the reproducible and place them in a folder at the center. If students will respond in their notebooks, make several task cards by laminating copies of the reproducible. Have them make the two-column chart shown on the task card.
2. Model the procedure before placing the activity at the center.

Procedure

1. In the first column of the reproducible (or in the organizer they've drawn in their notebooks), students draw or write what they see in their book's illustrations. In fiction, they can focus on the facial expressions of the characters, their actions, and the setting. In nonfiction, they can focus on the information contained within the photographs, diagrams, maps, and charts.
2. In the second column, students list the connections they make from their own experience (what they know) to their notes about characters, setting, story events, or topics from the first column.

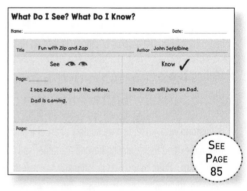

Activity 2

Connection Stems

Purpose: Students will connect their lives to a story or nonfiction text.

Materials

- Picture-Cued Connection Stems reproducible (page 86)
- scissors, paper clips
- can, twin pocket folder or desktop pocket chart
- student notebooks or writing paper

Preparation

1. Make copies of the reproducible on card stock.
2. Cut each copy into separate strips; students can take a set of strips to their seats and place each strip directly above their recording page for ease of copying. Store the sets of strips in a can, desktop pocket chart, or twin pocket folder at the center.

Tip

Different reading materials will elicit different types of responses. Not every book is humorous and not every book causes a reader to respond both emotionally (I feel) and intellectually (I think), so a degree of open-endedness in this task is necessary.

Tip

To create a simple two-column chart in a notebook, see page 73.

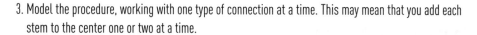

3. Model the procedure, working with one type of connection at a time. This may mean that you add each stem to the center one or two at a time.

Procedure

1. Students select a sentence stem to complete (or take one that has been assigned) to help them respond to an independent-reading book.

2. They copy the stem into their notebook or onto a sheet of paper and then complete it with their connection.

Modeling Tips

Remind students that they can make connections to their own lives, to books or movies, or to community or world events. Demonstrate several different ways to respond each time you introduce a connection stem.

I n t e r m e d i a t e L e v e l

Activity 1
What I Think

Purpose: Students will make connections to a character and events in a story or to the topic and facts in a nonfiction text.

Materials

- What I Think reproducible (page 87)
- folder or student notebooks

Preparation

1. For individual response sheets, make copies of the reproducible and place them in a folder at the center. If students will respond in their notebooks, make several task cards by laminating copies of the reproducible.

2. Model how to use this graphic organizer before assigning it as center work.

Procedure

On the reproducible or in their notebooks, students fill in the organizer, describing the connections they make to the character or topic and events or facts.

Modeling Tips

1. Use these guiding questions as you think aloud about your own connections.

- **Character:** How is the character like or not like me in terms of character traits?

- **Topic:** What have I heard or read about this topic? How does this topic relate to my life?

- **Events:** Has something similar happened to me? Would I do and say the same things these characters did in this book, or would I behave differently? Have I ever experienced a problem like this one? How would I go about solving it?

- **Facts:** What responses do I have to these ideas or facts? What connections do I make to what I already know? What new information have I learned?

2. Address students' difficulties in making connections. This challenge may arise when students' life experiences and personality traits may be very different from those of the characters and topics in their reading. Or they may lack background knowledge to help them relate to ideas, objects, and events in the text. It is important to explain that this does sometimes happen and to model how to record the reasons why it was difficult to make a connection.

Activity 2
In the Driver's Seat

Purpose: Students will make connections and self-monitor for understanding.

Materials

- In the Driver's Seat reproducible (page 88)
- folder or student notebooks

Preparation

1. For individual response sheets, make copies of the reproducible and place them in a folder at the center. If students will respond in their notebooks, make several task cards by laminating copies of the reproducible.
2. Read aloud a short passage and describe the connections you make to the character or topic. Point out any roadblocks that stood in the way of your comprehension. These may include a confusing event, fact or idea, a word you do not know, and complex language structures. Model several strategies to clarify these, such as rereading, reading on, thinking about what you already know and what would make sense, looking inside the word for parts you know, and examining the pictures. Explain that identifying what you understand and what you don't and then trying to make sense of the confusing parts are skills all good readers use.

Procedure

1. Students self-monitor for understanding by describing connections they made to the character or topic. They also share their prior knowledge about the topic.
2. Next, students identify the parts of the reading that they found confusing or puzzling.
3. Students fill in the graphic organizer, recording their responses on the reproducible or in their notebooks.

Advanced Level

Activity 1
Build a Connection

Purpose: Students will connect their reading to their life experiences, other books they have read or listened to, and events or issues in the world around them.

Materials

- Build a Connection reproducible (page 89)
- card stock and glue stick
- student notebooks

Preparation

1. Make copies of the reproducible on card stock and laminate to create task cards. If you wish to have students work on only one of the three types of connections at a time, make a task card for each section: Cut the chart apart, glue the three sections onto separate sheets of card stock, laminate the sheets, and present one at a time in consecutive center rotations.
2. Model each type of connection before assigning it as center work.

Procedure

1. Assign, or have students choose, one type of connection from the chart (text to self, text to text, and text to world).

2. Students choose a sentence stem listed for the connection they've chosen and use it to help them write a connection.

Note: Not all reading material will lend itself to text-to-world connections, so be sure to offer some flexibility unless the reading material provided at the center has been specifically chosen to support this type of connection (for example, a magazine article on recycling or a nonfiction reader on an endangered animal).

Guided Practice Tips

- Model the procedure using a book for which students have copies. After the first reading, have students place a sticky note on pages you have designated as stopping points during the reading and invite them to share the connections they have made to the text up to that point. They may share these with a partner or record them on an individual whiteboard to share with the group in a "show up" format where every student holds up his or her whiteboard to the group or a partner at the same time.

- For the next section of the reading, have students select their own stopping points during their reading. Give them a target number of stops to make by limiting the number of sticky notes you provide to two or three. Allow time for them to share their connections again.

Activity 2
Tic-Tac-Connect

Purpose: Students will connect prior knowledge and life experiences to the reading.
.

Materials

- Tic-Tac-Connect reproducible (page 90)
- card stock
- student notebooks

Preparation

1. Copy the reproducible onto card stock to make the Tic-Tac-Connect board. Make one board for every student (or for every two students if students will work in pairs).
2. Model the procedure in a whole-group or small-group setting before assigning the task at the center.

Procedure

1. Students select three picture-cued connection prompts from the grid.
2. Students copy each connection prompt in their notebooks and write or draw their connection to the independent reading material.

Extension

This can be used in a game format for two students who have read the same book. Player X takes a square by making a connection in response to the prompt in that space. The next turn goes to player Y, who must make a connection in response to the prompt in the square he or she chooses. Players must take a total of three squares in a row, across, down, or diagonally.

Read, Relate, Respond

Name: _____ Date: _____

Title _____ Author _____

Wow! This part is exciting.	This is puzzling.
I think . . .	I feel . . .
A funny part is . . .	A surprising part is . . .

What Do I See? What Do I Know?

Name: _____

Date: _____

Title _____ Author _____	
See 👁👁	**Know** ✓
Page: _____	
Page: _____	

Connection Stems

I can . . .

If I were . . .

This is like the time when . . .

I read . . .

I saw . . .

I know . . .

In the world . . .

Differentiated Literacy Centers © 2007 by Margo Southall, Scholastic Teaching Resources page 86

What I Think

Name: _____   Date: _____

Title _____   Author _____

This is About	It Makes Me Think About
Who or What	
Events or Facts ✓	

In the Driver's Seat

Name: _____ Date: _____

Title _____

Author _____

Yes	No
A part I made connections to was . . . . I understood these facts or ideas	A part that was puzzling to me was . . . .

Build a Connection

  Text-to-Self Connections

- When I saw the picture of _____ I remembered . . .

- This part is like my life because . . .

- This character reminds me of myself because . . .

 Text-to-Text Connections

- This book is like _____ because . . .
  [title of another book]

- This character is like _____ in the
  [character]
  book _____ because . . .
  [title]

  Text-to-World Connections

- I saw something like this when I watched/read

  _____. What I know is . . .
  [newspaper, TV, movie]

- This reminds me of something that happened in the real world:

Differentiated Literacy Centers © 2007 by Margo Southall, Scholastic Teaching Resources page 89

Tic-Tac-Connect

Title: _____

Author: _____

Choose three connection starters across or down. Write a connection you made for each one.

Differentiated Literacy Centers © 2007 by Margo Southall, Scholastic Teaching Resources page 90

Generating and Answering Questions

Overview of Activities: Generating and Answering Questions				
Topic	**Activity**	**Level**	**Page**	**Repro**
Generating and Answering Questions	• Partner Quiz	M	92	99
	• I Wonder	B	93	100
	• I See, I Wonder	B	93	101
	• Who or What Am I?	I	94	102
	• Sticky Questions	I	94	—
	• Tic-Tac-Question #1 & #2	I	96	103, 104
	• Questions and Answers	I	96	—
	• What Kinds of Questions Do They Ask?	A	97	105
	• Tic-Tac-Question #3	A	97	106
	• Roll Up a Question	A	98	106

Generating questions as we read supports active thinking during the reading process (McLaughlin, 2003). The purpose of this center is to promote strategies for both generating and answering the questions that arise during reading—and by doing so, to keep our readers engaged and aware of their learning.

Teaching Tips for the Generating and Answering Questions Activities

- Introduce the questioning strategy with open-ended "Do you wonder . . .?" questions. This is a risk-free activity for struggling readers as there is no one right answer. Invite students to brainstorm "I wonder" statements when reading on class topics and themes.

- To encourage interaction, provide a plastic microphone for students to pass around as they generate questions. Record student questions on sentence strips and display these on a bulletin board, or on a chart for display, compile a list of questions about the topic or story. Use these as a focus for ongoing class research.

- Model and practice generating questions at the literal, inferential, and evaluative level during whole-class and small-group reading experiences. Use the same picture cues and terminology as the students have used in the center activities so that they may transfer their learning to independent learning contexts. Select the level of task for individual students according to the appropriate degree of complexity (for example, "how," "why," and "should" questions generally require a higher level of analysis than literal "who," "what," and "where" questions).

- Display question starters on a poster or 9- by 3-inch cards in a pocket chart so that students can refer to the prompts as a guide when they generate questions about their reading. Some of these question starters help students make sense of fiction, while others are more appropriate for nonfiction. Provide sentence starters for both fiction and nonfiction so that students can select those that best meet the text structure of their reading material. For questions about fiction, focus on story structure. For questions about nonfiction, focus on locating important information. These range from simple ("What is the name of the best friend in the story?") to more complex ("Why are Amy and Lina such good friends?").

> "Teaching students to ask their own questions improves their active processing of the text and their comprehension." (Put Reading First, 2001)

Activities

Partner Quiz

Purpose: Students will generate and answer questions in a cooperative learning context.

Materials

- Picture Question Cards reproducible (page 99)

- toy microphone (available from toy stores and resource catalogues)

- two copies of the same text or a partner reading book

- student notebooks (if a product is required)

Preparation

1. Make several copies of the reproducible on card stock and cut out the individual cards. Put the sets of cards into small resealable plastic bags or clip them together with an O-ring.
2. Provide a toy microphone and two copies of the same text at the center.
3. Model the procedure during a class read-aloud or shared reading by pausing at different points and having students turn to a partner and ask a question about the part you just read. Display enlarged copies of the Picture Question Cards or provide partners with a set of cards on an O-ring to support this activity

Procedure

1. Students read a copy of the same text either independently or as partners.
2. Students play the role of a quiz show host or TV reporter and use the prompts on the cards to help them question each other about the reading. Each partner may take one turn questioning and the next turn answering. If partners have trouble coming up with a question for the chosen prompt, they may help each other.
3. If you wish to evaluate a product for this task, ask students to record one of their questions and the answer their partner provided in their notebooks.

Modeling Tips

Each picture cue represents a specific type of question. The "why" and "how" questions sometimes require higher-level thinking and integration of information. Students may not find these answers spelled out in the text. Have students role-play a detective (fiction) or scientist (nonfiction) as they ask a partner a question about the class read-aloud. Use these question starters and the story elements or information they refer to as a guide to generating questions with a think-aloud:

- **Who:** The main character or topic of the book

- **What:** Events in the story or facts about the topic

- **Where:** The setting for the story or the geographic location of or environment surrounding the topic

- **When:** Time in which the events take place or the topic that is presented

- **Why:** This can refer to a number of possibilities, such as why did the character act and speak that way? Why did a specific event occur? Why do these animals behave this way? and other "detective" (fiction) or "super scientist" (nonfiction) questions.

- **How:** How was the problem in the story or a problem that has to do with the topic solved? A nonfiction example might include a possible solution to the problem of an endangered animal or other community and / or world issue.

Beginner Level

Activity 1
I Wonder

Purpose: Students will generate questions using picture-cued sentence stems.

Materials
- I Wonder reproducible (page 100)
- scissors
- student notebooks
- card stock
- small, resealable plastic bags, O-ring, or cube

Preparation
1. Make several copies of the reproducible on card stock. Cut each copy into separate strips; students can take a set of prompts to their seats and place each strip directly above their recording page for ease of copying. (Store the sets of strips in a can, desktop pocket chart, or twin-pocket folder at the center.)
2. Model the procedure by generating questions with a think-aloud based on a class read-aloud or shared reading. Write the "I wonder" prompts on sentence strips and have students generate questions about the reading using the prompts. (This could be a think-pair-share activity with students sharing in partners.) Introduce one or two question prompts at a time, and add each prompt to the center only after students have worked with it. You may need to work with one type of question at a time. This may mean that you add each stem to the center one or two at a time.

Procedure
1. Students select a prompt from the set.
2. Students use the prompt to write an "I wonder" sentence about an independent-reading book.
3. You may require students to generate a specific number of "I wonder" statements and to read these to a teammate.

Modeling Tips: (See tips for the Partner Quiz activity on page 92.)

Activity 2
I See, I Wonder

Purpose: Students will generate questions using visual information in the text, including illustrations and photos.

Materials
- I See, I Wonder reproducible (page 101)
- folder or student notebooks

Preparation
1. For individual response sheets, make copies of the reproducible and place them in a folder at the center. If students will respond in their notebooks, make several task cards by laminating copies of the reproducible. Have them make the two-column chart shown on the task card.
2. Model the procedure using the visual information in a big book.
3. To support emergent readers, provide the sentence starter "I wonder" prompts (page 100) to help them complete a written question.

Procedure

Students fill in the graphic organizer, recording their responses on the reproducible or in their notebooks.

- In the first column, students draw or write what they see in the book's illustrations and record the page number. For a fiction book, they can focus on the facial expressions of the characters, their actions, and the setting. For a nonfiction text, they can focus on the information contained within the photographs, diagrams, maps, and charts.
- In the second column, students list the questions they have about the character, setting, story events, or information.

Activity 3
Who or What Am I?

Purpose: Students will generate clues in the form of questions about story characters, settings, important objects, or factual information.

Materials
- Who or What Am I? reproducible (page 102)
- copy paper
- card stock

Preparation
1. Make several copies of the reproducible on card stock to serve as task cards.
2. Provide copy paper for the activity at the center.
3. Using a riddle format, model how to generate questions and answers about characters, settings, and important objects in stories. For generating and answering questions on information in nonfiction texts, use a trivia-game or game-show format.
4. To support emergent readers at the center, provide sentence starters based on the structure used in familiar riddle-books for the clues and answers, including the following:
   - It is . . .
   - I am a . . .
   - I can . . .
   - I eat . . .
   - I live . . .

Procedure
1. Using the examples provided on the form, students generate three clues about a character, setting, or important object in a story or about an important fact in a nonfiction text. (You may want to assign the text or have them choose their own, depending on the amount of support they will need.)
2. Students fold a sheet of copy paper in half to make a booklet. They write their clues on the cover and their answer on the inside. Encourage them to illustrate the answer as well.
3. Students read their riddle card to a partner at the center or during whole-class sharing.
4. Vary the focus story element or source of information each center rotation.

Intermediate Level

Activity 1
Sticky Questions

Purpose: Students will record questions during the reading.

Materials
- sticky notes or sticky flags
- student notebooks

Preparation

1. Have students make a simple two-column chart in their notebooks labeled "Sticky Stops / My Questions" to record an ongoing log of questions they make as they read.

Sticky Stops	My Questions
Page __4__	1. What kind of farm is it?
Page __12__	2. Do pigs just eat corn?

2. Provide sticky notes for students to use. Have students print a question mark on the notes if you wish to make the activity open-ended. You may also print with permanent marker on reusable sticky flags specific question-starting words, such as why and how, as well as short phrases (see those listed on the tic-tac-question grid, page 103, to guide the types of questions students generate).

3. During both shared and small-group reading contexts, show students how to place this focusing tool in the text alongside a part where you have a question. Be sure to demonstrate different levels of questions (literal, inferential, evaluative).

Procedure

1. Students select their own stopping points during their reading to generate questions. When they find a spot in the text where they have a question, they post a sticky note (or flag labeled with a question word) in the outside margin. If this activity is completed using guided reading text, you may suggest stopping points during the lesson and have students place the sticky notes or flags on those pages before they go to centers.

2. When they finish reading, students review the parts they marked. On the chart in their notebooks, they record the page number and the questions they generated.

Modeling Tips

- During a read-aloud, pause after the first page or paragraph and generate a question based on what you have read so far (for example, "What is puzzling at this point of the reading?" "What do we want to find out next?").
- Continue to model by pausing at the middle of the reading, when the problem has not yet been solved (fiction text) or all the information shared (nonfiction text). What does the reader hope to find out in the last section of the reading?
- Finally, pause at the end of the story or informational text. Are there any unanswered questions? Was the ending of the story satisfying or is there something the author left unsaid? What more do students want to find out about the nonfiction topic?
- After you've modeled the procedure, have students place a sticky note on pages you have designated as stopping points during the first part of the reading and share the questions they have made to the text up to that point.
- As you read the next section of text, make it more open-ended by having students mark the places they choose in the text where they have questions with sticky notes. Then allow them to share these with the group or a partner.

Guided Practice Tip

Repeat the modeling process with a second reading. Stop at several points and have students record their questions on a sticky note or whiteboard at each stopping point during the reading and share the

Tip

After sticky notes have been used to mark an important part of the book, they can be stored along the outside edge of a rectangular piece of laminated card stock for later use.

question with a partner. In a small group context have students select their own stopping places to mark with a sticky note. Ask them to share their question and read aloud a part that generated the question.

Activities 2 and 3
Tic-Tac-Question #1 and #2

Purpose: Students will generate literal and inferential questions.

Materials
- Tic-Tac-Question #1 and #2 reproducible (pages 103 and 104)
- card stock
- student notebooks

Preparation
1. Make several copies of each reproducible on card stock to create the tic-tac-question boards.
2. Model how to respond to each prompt. (You may want to introduce the literal-level prompts first (tic-tac-question #1) and the more challenging prompts (tic-tac-question #2) second, assigning one board at a time.
3. Review the procedure, showing students how to select three prompts in a row (across, down, or diagonally).

Procedure
1. Using the tic-tac-question board, students select three question prompts in a row.
2. In their notebooks, students copy the three prompts and write their questions about their reading.

Extension
This can be used in a game format for two students who have read the same book. (See extension idea for Tic-Tac-Connect, page 83.)

Activity 4
Questions and Answers

Purpose: Students will generate inferential and evaluative questions and answer these based on the clues the author has provided, as well as their own background knowledge, ideas, and opinions.

Materials
- Student notebooks

Preparation
1. Have students create a two-column chart in their notebooks labeled "My Questions / My Answers."
2. Model the procedure in a whole-group or small-group setting.

My Questions	My Answers
Page _5_ 1. Why does Charlie the cat like Elizabeth's bed?	1. She doesn't bother him.
Page _23_ 2. Why does he have two homes?	2. He loves both families.

Procedure
1. In the first column of the graphic organizer, students write a question they have about the reading that cannot be answered directly in the book. In the second column, students record a possible answer based on the clues in the book and their own background knowledge, ideas, and opinions.

Activity 1
What Kinds of Questions Do They Ask?

Purpose: Students will generate literal, inferential, and evaluative questions using picture cues.

Materials
- What Kinds of Questions Do They Ask? reproducible (page 105)
- Optional: Writing paper or student notebook
- card stock, gluestick

Preparation
For individual response sheets, make copies of the reproducible and place them in a folder at the center. If students will respond in their notebooks, make several task cards by laminating copies of the reproducible.
- Model the four types of questions by pausing at different points of a shared reading to generate each type of question.

Procedure
1. Students use the character picture cues for each of the types of questions to generate a question.
2. Students write their questions on the reproducible or in their notebooks.

Modeling Tip
Include questions that can be answered by:
- locating the answer in the book, as a robot would (for example "Who is the main character?" and "Where does the story take place?" or "Where is this happening?")
- using the clues the author has provided at different points in the book together with what you already know, as a detective would (for example, "Why does this character act this way at the beginning, but not at the end?")
- extending on the events or information in the book with a plan for a sequel or next step, or identifying a way of using the ideas or information, as a scientist or inventor would (for example, "How could we use paper products less so that we cut down fewer trees?")
- forming an opinion or evaluating the actions or ideas that are represented in this text based on your background knowledge and experience about the world, as a judge (for example, "Do you think Junie should have told the secret? Was the author right to risk the lives of the sled dogs in the race? Why or why not?")

Activity 2
Tic-Tac-Question #3

Purpose: Students will generate inferential and evaluative questions.

Materials
- Tic-Tac-Question #3 reproducible (page 106)
- student notebooks
- card stock

Preparation
1. Make several copies of the reproducible on card stock to create the tic-tac-question boards.
2. Model how to respond to each prompt.
3. Review the procedure, showing students how to select three prompts in a row (across, down, or diagonally).

Procedure

1. Students select three question prompts in a row to generate questions about their reading.
2. In their notebooks, students copy the prompt and write their questions about the text.

Extension

This can be used in a game format for two students who have read the same book. (See extension idea for Tic-Tac-Connect, page 83.)

Activity 3
Roll Up a Question

Purpose: Students will generate and answer inferential and evaluative questions.

Materials
- Tic-Tac-Question #3 reproducible (page 106)
- student notebooks
- cube

Preparation

1. Copy the reproducible onto card stock, cut apart the six pictures, and attach one to each side of the cube (simple cube-making ideas are included on page 67).
2. Model the procedure of turning the cube to select a specified number of prompts and use these to write a question and an answer. (Be sure that students have practice responding to each of the six prompts.)

Procedure

1. Students roll or turn the cube to select question prompts.
2. In their notebooks, students copy the prompt and write their questions and answers about their reading.

Extensions

This can be used in a game format for two students who have read the same text: Partners may take turns rolling the cube and generating questions for each other to answer.

To increase the challenge, use a die and the cube together: Students roll the die and then generate the number of questions indicated. For example, if a student tosses the die for a 3, he or she must roll the cube three times and generate a question for each question-starter prompt. Other question phrases to add to their list include:

- What might have caused . . . ?
- Would it be better if . . . ?
- What would you do if . . . ?
- How might . . . ?
- Who might . . . ?
- Do you agree that . . . ?

Picture Question Cards

Who? 	What? 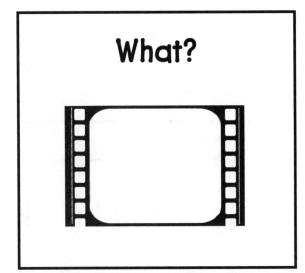
Where? 	Why? 
When? 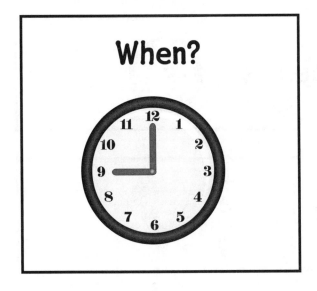	How? 

I Wonder

I wonder who . . .

I wonder what . . .

I wonder where . . .

I wonder why . . .

I wonder when . . .

I wonder how . . .

Differentiated Literacy Centers © 2007 by Margo Southall, Scholastic Teaching Resources page 100

I See, I Wonder

Name: _____ Date: _____

Title _____ Author _____

I See 👁👁	I Wonder ❓
Page: _____	
Page: _____	

Who or What Am I?

1. Use the book you read to write a riddle about:
   - A person or animal
   - A place
   - An important thing

2. On the cover write three clues about the person, animal, place, or thing you chose.

3. On the inside write and draw the answer. EXAMPLES:

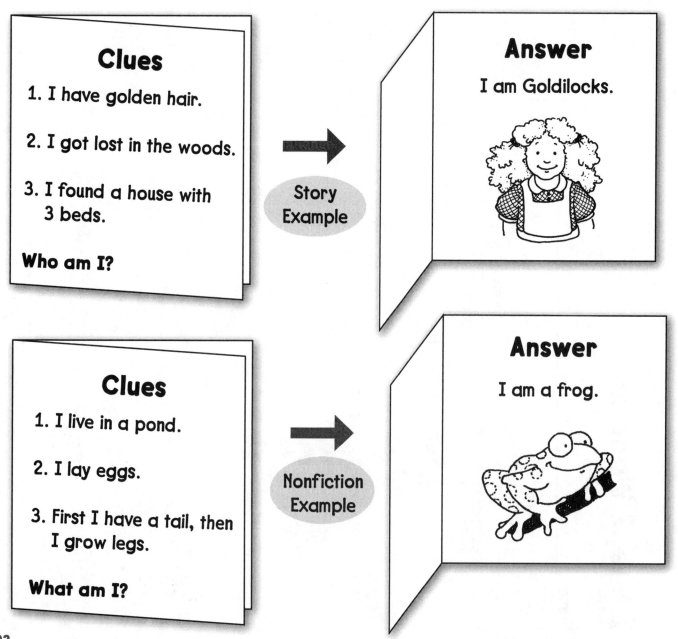

Clues

1. I have golden hair.

2. I got lost in the woods.

3. I found a house with 3 beds.

Who am I?

Story Example

Answer

I am Goldilocks.

Clues

1. I live in a pond.

2. I lay eggs.

3. First I have a tail, then I grow legs.

What am I?

Nonfiction Example

Answer

I am a frog.

Differentiated Literacy Centers © 2007 by Margo Southall, Scholastic Teaching Resources page 102

Tic-Tac-Question #1

Title: _____

Author: _____

Choose three question starters across, down, or diagonally. Think of a question that begins with these words.

Who is/are . . . ?	What did . . . ?	Where is/are . . . ?
?	?	?
Where did . . . ?	Who did . . . ?	What can . . . ?
?	?	?
What is . . . ?	Where can . . . ?	Who can . . . ?
?	?	?

Differentiated Literacy Centers © 2007 by Margo Southall, Scholastic Teaching Resources page 103

Tic-Tac-Question #2

Title: _____

Author: _____

Choose three question starters across, down, or diagonally. Think of a
question that begins with these words.

When is/are . . . ?	Why did . . . ?	How is/are . . . ?
?	?	?
How did . . . ?	When did . . . ?	Why can . . . ?
?	?	?
Why is . . . ?	How can . . . ?	When can . . . ?
?	?	?

Differentiated Literacy Centers © 2007 by Margo Southall, Scholastic Teaching Resources page 104

What Kinds of Questions Do They Ask?

Title: _____   Author: _____

Think of a question that each of these four characters would ask:

1. **Robot:** I can find the answer quickly on one page.

2. **Detective:** I will look in more than one place for clues to the answer.

3. **Judge:** I will give my opinion about what happened.

4. **Inventor:** I will think about how I would use this information.

Tic-Tac-Question #3

Title: _____

Author: _____

Choose three question starters across, down, or diagonally. Think of a question that begins with these words.

Why do you think . . . ? ?	**What might happen if . . . ?** ?	**How would you . . . ?** ?
Were they right to . . . ? ?	**What is the difference between . . . ?** ?	**Should . . . ?** ?
Why does . . . ? ?	**How could . . . ?** ?	**How do . . . ?** ?

Retelling and Summarizing

Overview of Activities: Retelling and Summarizing				
Topic	**Activity**	**Level**	**Page**	**Repro**
Retelling and Summarizing	• Stop, Draw, and Write	M	108	—
	• Retelling Flap Book	B	108	113
	• Retelling Cube for Stories	B	109	114
	• Retelling Cube for Facts	B	109	115
	• Character Close Up	I	110	116
	• Tic-Tac-Tell for Stories	I	110	117
	• Tic-Tac-Tell for Facts	I	111	118
	• Pyramid Summary	A	111	119
	• Partner Quiz Cards	A	112	120
	• Roll and Respond Cube	A	112	121

Retelling of a narrative text provides a focus for students as they recall important events in sequence, and, even more importantly, make causal connections between events. An expository retelling requires students to accurately record facts, and to determine key information to remember.

Learning to retell skillfully requires regular practice and is a daily activity in many primary classrooms. You can provide three levels of support to help students complete a retelling. The first level is a guided oral retelling during which you model parts of the retelling and have students fill in important elements. The second level is a scaffolded assignment in which students complete a graphic organizer that prompts them to provide needed information. The third level is an independent, written retelling by students (Flynt & Cooter, 2005). Students need ample practice at the first two levels before they can be expected to write a coherent, sequential, and complete retelling.

The activities in this chapter not only give students practice with these detailed retellings, but also with more concise summaries that give an overview of the reading. Both skills are needed to enhance student's ability to understand the whole text—the organization of its details as well as the big picture.

Teaching Tips

- Introduce the strategy of summarizing by orally summing up a familiar story or movie in one or two sentences or read the summaries of familiar books on the back covers. You can model the process of retelling by recording the events in sequence in a comic-strip format on a chart or overhead transparency. Draw students' attention to the fact that the summary tells only the most important events or ideas.

- To illustrate the difference between a retelling and a summary you may create a two-column chart with the headings "Retelling" and "Summary" and have students tell all they can remember about the read-aloud, recording this in the first column. Review these story elements (fiction) or facts (nonfiction) and identify one to three events or facts that are important ("What does the author want us to remember most?"). You may place a sticky note on the outside of the chart alongside these key events or facts or draw a star beside them. Work with students to combine this information in one or two sentences and record them in the second column under the heading "Summary" (see more in the section Evaluating and Determining Importance, page 122).

"There is ample research indicating that practice in retelling improves not only retelling itself but students' ability to answer questions." (Caldwell & Leslie, 2005)

Activities

Multilevel

Stop, Draw, and Write

Purpose: Students will record the events in a story or information in a nonfiction text using illustrations.

Materials
- student notebooks or copy paper
- pencils

Preparation
1. Have students fold their notebook page to the center to form a two-column graphic organizer.
2. Model the procedure with a read aloud, pausing at stopping places in the text to sketch an event or fact in the first column and write a summary in the second column.
3. Demonstrate how to add more detail to each successive sketch as you learn more about the story or topic.

Procedure
1. In the first column of the reproducible, students draw the events and information in the first part of their reading. This is a simple pencil sketch, not an elaborate illustration. No coloring pencils are used.
2. In the second column, students write a summary describing the event or information they have sketched.

Beginner Level

Activity 1
Retelling Flap Book

Purpose: Students will identify the character, setting, and main event(s) in a story.

Materials
- Retelling Flap Book reproducible (page 113)
- scissors

Preparation
1. Make copies of the reproducible. Fold each sheet along the vertical fold line to form a booklet and cut along the two dotted lines from the edge to the center (fold line). This creates a three-part flapbook.
2. Model the procedure of recording the character, setting, and main event(s) under the corresponding picture cue.

Procedure
1. Under the first flap, students write about and/or draw the main character
2. Under the second flap, students write about and/or draw the setting.
3. Under the third flap, students write about and/or draw the main event(s).

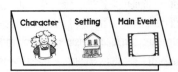 

Activity 2
Retelling Cube for Stories

Purpose: Students will retell the central elements of a story (story structure).

Materials
- Retelling Cube for Stories reproducible (page 114)
- Small, resealable plastic bags (or O-rings) or cube
- student notebooks
- scissors
- glue (cube option)

Preparation
1. Make several copies of the reproducible on card stock and cut out the individual cards. Put each set of cards into a small resealable bag (or hole punch the top corner of each card and clip the set together with an O-ring).
2. For a cube format, copy the reproducible onto card stock, cut apart the six pictures, and attach them to the six sides of the cube (simple cube-making ideas are included on page 67).
3. Model how to use the six question cards to guide a narrative summary:
   - Who is the main character?
   - Where does the story take place?
   - What does the character want? What is his or her goal?
   - What is the problem?
   - What is the solution?
   - How does the story end?

Procedure
1. Students use the prompt cards to retell the story, either orally, in written form, or both. Students turn the cube or use the set of cards to select the number of prompts you have specified for this activity.
2. To support emergent readers, you may require only an oral retelling. If students are writing, you may want them to write their answers to the questions in list form. Later, you may be able to model how to pull the answers together in a two- or three-sentence summary.
3. Students can use the prompt cards with a partner, each orally retelling their own story or one they both read before writing a retelling. Each student will take turns to question one another, so that together they use all of the prompts.

Activity 3
Retelling Cube for Facts

Purpose: Students will retell the key information in a nonfiction text.

Materials
- Retelling Cube for Facts reproducible (page 115)
- small, resealable plastic bags (or O-rings) or cube
- student notebooks
- scissors
- glue (cube option)

Preparation
1. See Preparation for Retelling Cube for Stories above to create prompt card sets or a cube.
2. Model using the picture-cued prompts to summarize the key information from a nonfiction text.

Procedure
1. Students select a prompt card and respond to the prompt. Alternatively, they roll or turn the cube and respond to the prompt on the top face of the cube. (The number of prompts you wish students to complete—two or three, for example—will determine the number of cube rolls or cards students may take.)

2. You may also require students to use the prompts with a partner to orally retell a story they have both read before writing a retelling. Each student will take turns to question his or her partner, so that together they use all of the prompts

Extension

Students use the cards in a collaborative game by turning over all the cards, taking turns picking one up, and using it to ask their partner a question about a story they have both read.

Intermediate Level

Activity 1
Character Close Up

Purpose: Students will identify the character's key actions and important comments and make inferences.

Materials
- Character Close Up reproducible (page 116)
- (optional) student notebooks
- folder

Preparation
1. For individual response sheets, make copies of the reproducible and place them in a folder at the center. If students will respond in their notebooks, make a task card with the reproducible.
2. Model how to use the prompts on the page with a think-aloud:
   - **Do:** What action did the character take to solve the problem or respond to a challenge? (Focus on one scene in which the character makes a key decision or responds in an important way to a situation.)
   - **Say:** What important words did this character say to another character during the event? Or make an inference about what the character might have said. (The comment you select should reflect a character trait, determine the next step in an adventure, or offer a solution to the problem.)
   - **Think:** What might the character have been thinking at that moment? (You'll need to make an inference using clues about the character's actions and words.)

Procedure
1. In the Do box, students record the character's action during a main event.
2. In the Say box, they record something important the character said or might have said during this event.
3. In the Think box, they write what the character might have been thinking at this moment.

Activity 2
Tic-Tac-Tell for Stories

Purpose: Students will retell the central elements of a story.

Materials
- Tic-Tac-Tell for Stories reproducible (page 117)
- student notebooks
- card stock

Preparation
1. Copy the reproducible onto card stock to make the tic-tac-tell board.
2. Alternatively, cut out six of the prompts from the reproducible to create a cube (simple cube-making ideas are included on page 67), or hole-punch the top of each card and clip the cards together with an O-ring.

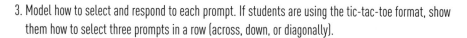

3. Model how to select and respond to each prompt. If students are using the tic-tac-toe format, show them how to select three prompts in a row (across, down, or diagonally).

Procedure
1. On the tic-tac-tell board, students select three prompts in a row. If they are using a cube, students roll or turn the cube to select several prompts.
2. Students write their response to the prompts in their notebooks.

Activity 3
Tic-Tac-Tell for Facts

Purpose: Students will retell the information in a nonfiction text and identify new information they have learned.

Materials
- Tic-Tac-Tell for Facts reproducible (page 118)
- student notebooks
- card stock

Preparation and Procedure
See Tic-Tac-Tell for Stories above. This activity is designed on the same principles, only it is to be used when the student has read a nonfiction text.

Advanced Level

Activity 1
Pyramid Summary

Purpose: Students will summarize the information in a nonfiction text and identify new information they have learned.

Materials
Pyramid Summary reproducible (page 111)

Preparation
1. For individual response sheets, make copies of the reproducible and place them in a folder at the center. If students will respond in their notebooks, make several copies of the reproducible on card stock to create task cards for the center. (If you laminate the task card, students can use dry-erase markers or crayons to answer on the form and then wipe away their response when they've finished.)
2. Model how to complete the pyramid organizer with words and phrases that represent the important information or events in a shared text. When you fill in the form, encourage them to begin with the topic and then follow with key facts on the following lines like so:

Example

```
                    Dinosaurs
                 Are      extinct
            Lived      long      ago
         Ate      meat      or      plants
    Fossils    tell    about    their    lives
```

Procedure:

1. In their notebooks or on copies of the reproducible, students complete a pyramid organizer with words that sum up the text. They write one word on the top line (it may be easiest for students to begin by naming the topic itself), a two-word phrase on the second line, a three-word phrase on the third line, and so on to concisely describe the topic. (For an additional challenge, they may use a prompt form such as the retelling cubes on pages 114 and 115 to make sure they've got all the elements of a summary.)

2. Students draw a triangle around the summary.

Activity 2
Partner Quiz Cards

Purpose: Students will use retelling and summarizing prompts to better understand a story or nonfiction book as they read it together.

Materials
- Partner Quiz Cards reproducible (page 120)
- scissors
- card stock
- student notebooks (optional)

Preparation
1. Copy the reproducible on card stock and cut out the individual cards to create sets.

Procedure
1. A pair of students reads two different texts or a common text at the center.
2. After they read a page or a section, one partner selects a quiz card and asks the other partner a question. The other partner answers. Then they read the next part or section and switch roles.
3. Option: Students may record both their question and their answer in their notebooks.

Activity 3
Roll and Respond Cube

Purpose: Students will use prompts to respond to a story or a nonfiction book.

Materials
- Roll and Respond Cube reproducible (page 121)
- cube
- student notebooks
- card stock
- scissors and glue

Preparation
1. Copy the reproducible onto card stock, cut apart the six pictures, and attach one to each side of the cube (simple cube-making ideas are included on page 67).
2. Have students practice each type of response in a small-group format before placing the cube at the center.

Procedure
1. Students roll or turn the cube and respond to the prompt on the top face of the cube. If they are using a task card, they choose a prompt. (The number of prompts you wish students to complete will determine the number of times they'll roll the cube.)
2. Students write their responses in their notebooks. You may require that students use the prompts with a partner to generate ideas about a story they have both read before they write a retelling. Each student will take turns to question his or her partner, so that together they use all of the prompts.

Retelling Flap Book

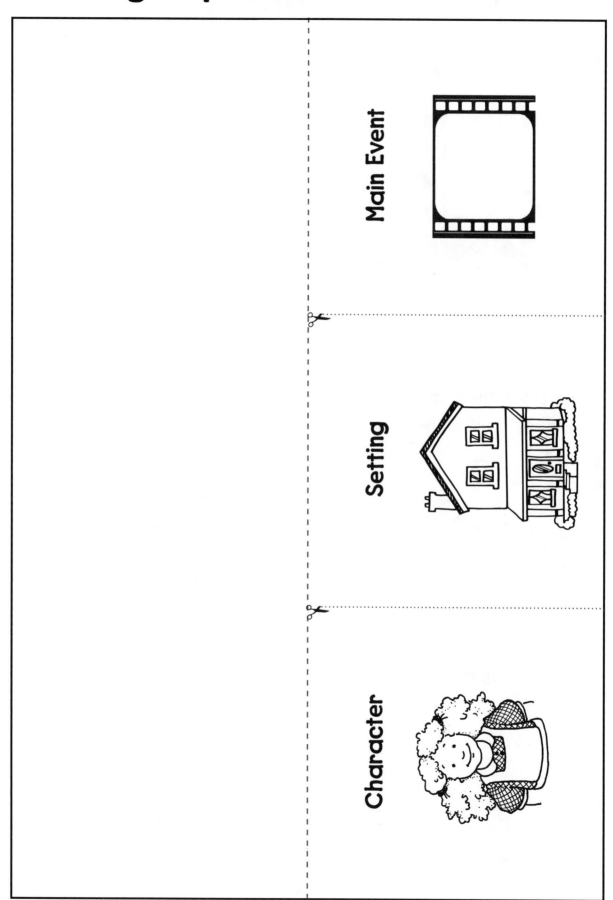

Main Event

Setting

Character

Retelling Cube for Stories

Who is the main character? 	**Where does the story take place?** 
What does the character want? What is his or her goal? 	**What is the problem?** 
What is the solution? 	**How does the story end?** 

Differentiated Literacy Centers © 2007 by Margo Southall, Scholastic Teaching Resources page 114

Retelling Cube for Facts

Tell all the facts like a robot.

Tell where and when this happens.

Tell 2 facts you knew before you read this book.

Tell it like the TV news: What happened? Why and how did it happen?

Tell how someone could use these facts.

Tell 2 new facts that you learned.

Character Close Up

Name: _____ Date: _____

Title: _____

Author: _____

Do

Say

Think

Tic-Tac-Tell for Stories

Title: _____

Author: _____

Choose three retelling starters across, down, or diagonally.

Tell how the character is like or not like someone you know. 	Describe the feelings the character showed in the story. 	Retell the important things the character said. 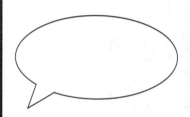
Pretend you are a detective. What are the clues that tell us where the story happened?	List the places where important events happened. 	Draw a map of the places where the story happened. 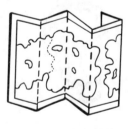
Draw a comic strip of three things that happened. 	Pretend you are the author. Tell the most exciting events. 	Write three events on sticky notes and put them in the right order. 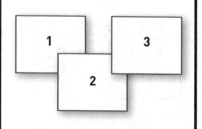

Tic-Tac-Tell for Facts

Title: _____

Author: _____

Choose three retelling starters across, down, or diagonally.

Pretend you are a robot. Tell just the facts. 	Write 2 new facts that you learned about this topic. 	Describe the most important thing the author wants us to remember. 
List the place(s) in the world this happens. 	Pretend you are a scientist. Plan how you will use these facts to try something new. 	Draw a picture of where this fits in your life. 
Draw a comic strip of three important facts. 	Pretend you are a reporter. Tell the interesting facts. 	Write three facts on sticky notes and put them in the right order. 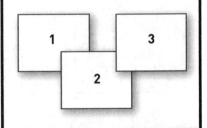

Pyramid Summary

Name: _____ Date: _____

Title: _____

Author: _____

- Summarize what you have read.

- Choose words and phrases that tell the important things to remember. Follow the pyramid format: Begin with one word, then two words, then three, and so on.

Partner Quiz Cards

 Partner Quiz

List the last three events or facts.

1 2 3

 Partner Quiz

Retell the story or nonfiction text so far.

First . . .   Next . . .

Then . . .   Finally . . .

Partner Quiz

Summarize the story or nonfiction text in one sentence.

 Tell who or what is involved, what happened, when and where it happened, and why.

Partner Quiz

What is the problem so far or what could be a problem?

 Partner Quiz

Explain a part that might be confusing.

Partner Quiz

Tell what caused something important to happen.

Partner Quiz

Imagine what would happen if someone or something important changed.

 **What if? . . .**

Partner Quiz

What do you think might happen next or what might be the next topic?

Roll and Respond Cube

Report an important event or fact. 	Ask a question about the character, topic, events, or facts. 
Point out an interesting or puzzling word. 	Share an interesting idea or fact. 
Tell about something you knew before reading. 	Explain something new you learned from the reading. 

Evaluating and Determining Importance

Overview of Activities: Evaluating and Determining Importance				
Topic	**Activity**	**Level**	**Page**	**Repro**
Evaluating, Determining Importance	• Reason to Read	M	123	—
	• Talk to the Author	B	123	127
	• Readers' Café	B	124	128
	• What's Most Important?	I	125	129
	• Star Review	I	125	130
	• Critic's Cube	A	126	131

Much of the difficulty students have with comprehension assessments is in the area of evaluative thinking, in which we ask them to go beyond retelling a series of events or answering a literal-level question. Evaluative tasks require them to make a judgment and justify their position (for example, "Do you agree that Fern should keep Wilbur as a pet, considering he is a farm animal? Explain your position."). Students need to be able to produce an opinion or judgment about specific aspects of the author's writing and also explain why they have come to this conclusion, by showing evidence from the text.

Teaching Tips

Teacher Modeling and Demonstration

● Introduce the strategy with some real-life examples of evaluative writing, such as a review of a trade book, movie, or sporting event in the newspaper. (You can find reviews of books on Web sites where children's books are sold as well as in education journals, which may be kept in your school library.) To have students exercise their evaluative skills, ask them to make a list ranking their top four favorite games, sports, foods, movies, or books, and share with the class why they placed their choices in this order. During a read-aloud, you can encourage younger children to use their evaluative skills by pausing to have them consider an event or decision that has caused a problem. Let them give a thumbs-up signal to show agreement or a thumbs-down signal to show disagreement with the way in which the character responded to a challenge or choice he or she made.

● During class shared-reading experiences, model how to establish a "dialogue with the author" and invite student input as you critique and make suggestions about the piece of literature you have just read together. Record student opinions and the reasons for these in simple two-column charts, labeled "Our Opinions / Why." Other charts can include a focus on specific aspects of the author's writing. Topics for discussion may include:
   ○ the unfolding story line (fiction) or coverage of the topic (nonfiction)
   ○ twist to a story or interesting information
   ○ specific writing techniques the author used, such as an action-packed opening or the use of illustrations to help tell the story
   ○ information they felt should have been included

Student Practice

● Book talks or reviews are an important source of ongoing modeling of this comprehension strategy. Provide a regularly scheduled time for students to recommend reading materials to one another. Set a time limit for stating what they liked about this book and why they might recommend it for others to read ("What are the hooks for this book?"). Have them explain their opinions and ideas about this reading. To help them prepare a thoughtful response, you might provide an outline, based on the categories you'll find in the following center activities.

- Let struggling readers and writers, and students who are less confident presenting to their peers, practice their review orally with a partner before sharing with the class. If a student feels more comfortable with prompts when he or she is talking, provide a sheet with picture-cued headings to help him or her remain on track and confident when standing in front of the class.

- Consider displaying some of the reviews children write for online book stores, such as Amazon, as a model for student critiques. Class surveys of favorite books, foods and activities can also provide samples of rating or ranking.

- In addition to book talks, students may write critiques of books on index cards to be displayed in the "Critics' Review Column" on the bulletin board. Draw attention to students' personal tastes in reading and maintain interest by having one student each week choose a selection of his or her favorites and put them on a book rack labeled with his or her name at the center.

Activities

Multilevel

Reason to Read

Purpose: Students use a persuasive voice to evaluate a story or nonfiction text.

Materials
- Copy paper and markers

Preparation
1. Show students several advertisements for children's toys. Discuss the use of persuasive language and images to convince a buyer of the value of the toy.
2. With the class create a model advertisement for a recent read-aloud book.

Procedure
Have students create an advertisement for their book using words and images. Ask them to consider:

- Why would they recommend this book to a friend?

- What are the most interesting events or questions that would attract another reader? What hooks can you use to grab their attention? Were there any amazing or surprising facts?

- Can you ask a question that will leave them wondering "What really happens?"—and a reason to read and find out?

Beginner Level

Activity 1
Talk to the Author

Purpose: Students will evaluate a piece of literature.

Materials

- Talk to the Author reproducible (page 127)
- student notebooks (optional)

Preparation

1. For individual response sheets, make copies of the reproducible and place them in a folder at the center. If students will respond in their notebooks, make several task cards by laminating copies of the reproducible.

2. Model the procedure by critiquing a short book you have read with the class and filling in the chart. For each section of the organizer, share one or two parts
   a. you enjoyed (fill in the "I agree" section)
   b. you thought were particularly powerful (fill in the "Great idea!" section)
   c. you thought could be improved with additional events or details ("I would change or add").
   Invite student input as you discuss each of the three aspects.

Procedure

Students fill in the graphic organizer, recording their responses on the reproducible or in their notebooks.

- In the first row, students describe and/or draw a part of the book they enjoyed, for example, the helpful way that the author organized the information, including maps, diagrams, and photos. They might also share an opinion the author gives that they agree with.
- In the second row, students identify a part they thought was outstanding. They give the author a compliment for this part of the writing.
- In the third row, students list something they would like to change or add about the book.

Activity 2
Readers' Café

Purpose: Students will evaluate a book's beginning, middle, and ending.

Materials

- Reader's Café reproducible (page 128)
- student notebooks (optional)

Preparation

1. For individual response sheets, make copies of the reproducible and place them in a folder at the center. If students will respond in their notebooks, make several task cards by laminating copies of the reproducible.

2. Model the procedure using the analogy of appetizer, main course, and dessert for the beginning, middle, and ending of a story.
   - Did the author catch and hold the reader's interest in the beginning and middle?
   - Was the ending satisfying or was something missing?

Use examples from books you have read aloud, pointing out the techniques that favorite authors have used to introduce the writing, how they "stretch out" a main event with dialogue, description, and detail, and the techniques they use to wrap up the story or informational piece, such as reflecting on the main event, making a decision or wish for the future (fiction), and restating the main idea/summarizing the facts (nonfiction).

Procedure

Students answer the questions, recording their responses on the reproducible or in their notebooks.

- In the first row (Appetizer section), they identify how the author got their attention in the beginning of the book.

- In the second row (Main Course section), they describe how the author included dialogue, action, and description to keep the reader's attention
- In the third row (Dessert section), they share how they felt about the ending of the book—whether they were satisfied or whether they thought something was missing

Intermediate

Activity 1
What's Most Important?

Purpose: Students will prioritize events or information and vocabulary.

Materials
- What's Most Important? reproducible (page 129)
- small resealable plastic bags
- student notebooks
- card stock
- index cards

Preparation
1. For individual response sheets, make copies of the reproducible and place them in a folder at the center. If students will respond in their notebooks, make several task cards by laminating copies of the reproducible. In this case, have students make a simple two-column chart in their notebooks labeled "Important / Most Important."
2. Model the procedure by listing the key words, events, or facts from a shared reading on sentence strips or large sticky notes. Set up a two-column chart labeled "Important / Most Important." Have students help you determine which events, facts, or words should be placed in the "Important" column of the chart. Guide students to discard any events, facts, or words that are minor details. Have students discuss the remaining "important" elements and select the two or three that seem most essential to helping us understand the story or nonfiction text. Move the sticky notes with these key events, facts, or words to the "Most Important" column.

Procedure
1. Students record on index cards three important events or facts and three words that represent key ideas or information about the story or text.
2. On the reproducible or in their notebook chart, students arrange the index cards in order of importance on the "Important" column. Then they select one word card and one event or fact card representing essential ideas and information that the story or text must have to be understood—and place these in the "Most Important" column.
3. Students copy the lists from each column on the reproducible or in their notebook charts.

Activity 2
Star Review

Purpose: Students will evaluate the author's writing and use of visuals (effect, clarity, and description).

Materials
- Star Review reproducible (page 130)

Preparation
1. Make copies of the reproducible and place them in a folder at the center.

2. Establish the criteria for rating a book from 1–4 stars. (Use criteria that are familiar to students, such as trait-based rubric criteria they use to evaluate their own writing.)

3. Model the procedure on a chart copy using student input. To evaluate the writing in a fictional text, discuss how well the author described the main character(s).

- Can you visualize them?
- Do you feel that you know them?
- Could you describe them to someone else?
- Are they real—could they be someone you know?

Next, evaluate the author's style. Does the author use words effectively to describe the action so that you can "see a movie in your mind"? For a nonfiction text, discuss the author's organization of the book, as well as the clarity of the facts and description. For both genres, examine the use of visual literacy, such as illustrations, photos, diagrams, maps and charts. How do they add to or support the author's words? Share examples from online book stores, such as Amazon, where children have posted their evaluations.

Procedure

1. Students rate the author's work on a scale of 1 to 4, coloring or circling the appropriate number of stars (for example, this may include his or her description of the main characters, word choice, overall structure, solution to the story's problem, and voice). Then they write an explanation justifying why they gave this rating.

2. In the second section, following the same procedure, students rate the author's use of illustrations or photos.

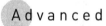

A d v a n c e d

Activity
Critic's Cube

Purpose: Students will use prompts to evaluate a fiction or nonfiction book.

Materials
- Critic's Cube reproducible (page 131)
- cube
- student notebooks
- card stock
- scissors and glue

Preparation

1. Copy the reproducible on card stock, cut apart the six cards, and attach one to each side of the cube (simple cube-making ideas are included on page 67). Alternatively, you can create card sets, storing the six cards in a resealable bag or hole-punching the top left corner and fastening the set with an O-ring.

2. During a read-aloud, model using each of the prompts to evaluate a story or nonfiction text.

Procedure

1. Students roll or turn the cube and respond to the prompt on the top face of the cube. If they are using a set of cards, they choose a prompt.

2. You may indicate the number of prompts you wish students to complete, or rolls of the cube, such as two or three.

3. Students write their responses in their notebooks.

4. This may be a collaborative activity in which students use the prompts with a partner before writing a summary or a retelling. Partners will take turns questioning each other, so that together they use all of the prompts.

Extension

This can be used in a game format for two students who have read the same book. (See extension idea for Tic-Tac-Connect, page 83.)

Talk to the Author

Name: _____   Date: _____

Title	Author
I agree 😊	
Great idea! 💡	
I would change or add ✏️	

Readers' Café

Name: _____ Date: _____

Title: _____

Author: _____

Read as a writer. Write as a reader.

Appetizer: What hooks did the author use to grab you in the **beginning** of this book?

_____

_____

_____

Main Course: How did the author keep you reading in the **middle** of the book? How did he or she s-t-r-e-t-c-h out the main event or make the facts interesting?

_____

_____

_____

Dessert: Did the author give you a satisfying **ending**? Was anything missing? What could they add?

_____

_____

_____

Differentiated Literacy Centers © 2007 by Margo Southall, Scholastic Teaching Resources page 128

What's Most Important?

Name: _____ Date: _____

Title: _____

Author: _____

1. Find all the important events (or facts) and words from your reading. Write these in the "Important" column.

2. Select one top word and one top event (or fact) and move them to the "Most Important" column.

Important ★ • Events and Words (Story) • Facts and Words (Nonfiction text)	Most Important ★ ★ ★ ★ • Events and Words (Story) • Facts and Words (Nonfiction text)

Star Review

Name: _____ Date: _____

Title: _____

Author: _____

Rate how well this book was written and presented.

Color the number of stars you think is a fair rating.

Writing:

Explain why with examples from the book.

_____

_____

_____

Pictures or Photos:

Explain why with examples from the book.

_____

_____

_____

Critics' Cube

Why do you think the author wrote this book? **What is the author trying to tell us?**	**What did the author need to know in order to write this book?**
What makes this book different from other books you have read? **Why is it special and worth reading?**	**How could you use the information in this book?** **Who should read this book?** **Would you recommend it to a friend? Why or why not?**
What other information or events could the author have added to this book?	**What other illustrations or photos could the author have added to this book?**

Comprehension Menu Cards

Connecting

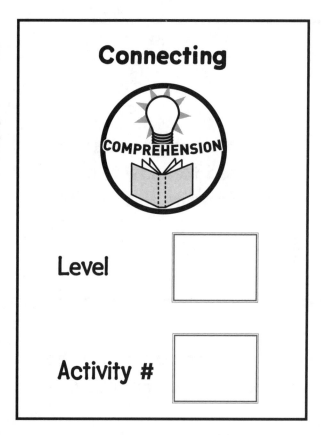

Level

Activity #

Questioning

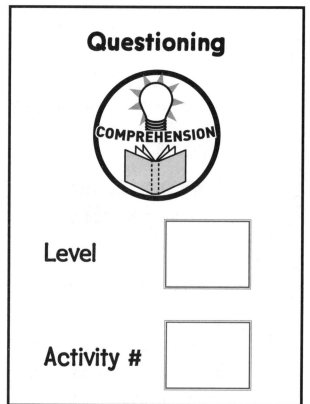

Level

Activity #

Retelling/Summarizing

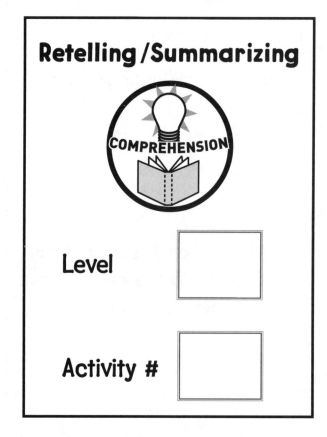

Level

Activity #

Evaluating

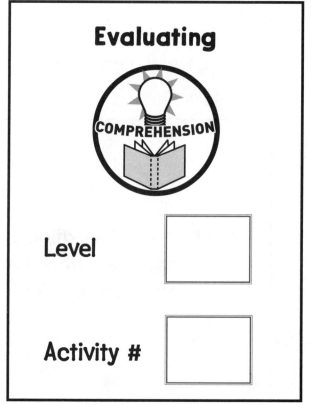

Level

Activity #

Making Connections: (Text to Self, Text to Text, Text to World)

17 Things I'm Not Allowed to Do Anymore by Jenny Offill and Nancy Carpenter (Schwartz & Wade Books, 2007)

A River Ran Wild by Lynne Cherry (Harcourt Brace Jovanovich, 1992)

Diary of a Worm by Doreen Cronin (Joanna Cotler Books)

Koala Lou by Mem Fox (Bayswater, Vic., 1988)

Wilfrid Gordon McDonald Partridge by Mem Fox (Kane / Miller Book Publishers, 1984)

Whoever You Are by Mem Fox (Harcourt Brace, 1997)

Today Was a Terrible Day by Particia Reilly Giff (Viking Press, 1980)

Julius, the Baby of the World by Kevin Henkes (Greenwillow Books, 1990)

The Younger Brother's Survival Guide by Lisa Kopelke (Simon & Schuster, 2006)

Hooway for Wodney Wat by Helen Lester (Houghton Mifflin, 1999)

What Are You So Grumpy About? by Tom Lichtenheld (Little, Brown and Co., 2003)

Treasures of the Heart by K.L. Darnell & Alice A. Miller (Sleeping Bear Press, 2003)

Oliver Button Is a Sissy by Tomie de Paola (Harcourt Brace Jovanovich, 1979)

What a Year! by Tomie de Paola (Putnam, 2002)

My Rotten Redheaded Older Brother by Patricia Polacco (Simon & Schuster, 1994)

The Relatives Came by Cynthia Rylant (Bradbury Press, 1985)

The Butter Battle Book by Dr. Seuss (Random House, 1984)

The Lorax by Dr. Seuss (Random House, 1971)

Alexander and the Terrible, Horrible, No Good, Very Bad Day by Judith Viorst (Atheneum, 1972)

39 Uses for a Friend by Harriet Ziefert (Putnam, 2001)

Questioning

Charlie Anderson by Barbara Abercrombie (M.K. McElderry Books, 1990)

The Lotus Seed by Sherry Garland (Harcourt Brace Jovanovich, 1993)

I Wonder by Tana Hoban (Harcourt Brace, 1999)

The Wise Woman and Her Secret by Eve Merriam (Aladdin, 1993)

The Three Questions by Jon J. Muth (Scholastic, 2002)

I Wonder Why series by Philip Steele (Kingfisher Publishing)

Gotta Go! Gotta Go! by Sam Swope (Farrar, Straus and Giroux, 2000)

An Interview With Harry the Tarantula by Leigh Ann Tyson (National Geographic, 2003)

Super Completely and Totally the Messiest by Judith Viorst (Atheneum Books for Young Readers, 2000)

Retelling and Summarizing

Magic School Bus series by Joanna Cole (Scholastic)

Once Upon a Cool Motorcycle Dude by Kevin O'Malley (Walker & Company, 2005)

The Paper Bag Princess by Robert Munsch (Annick Press, 1992)

The Frog Prince Continued by Jon Scieszka (Viking, 1991)

The Three Little Wolves and the Big Bad Pig by Eugene Trivizas (Simon & Schuster, 1997)

Evaluating / Determining What's Important

Two Bad Ants by Chris van Allsburg (Houghton Mifflin, 1988)

The Important Book by Margaret Wise Brown (Harper, 1949)

The Great Kapok Tree by Lynne Cherry (Harcourt Brace Jovanovich, 1990)

Hungry, Hungry Sharks by Joanna Cole (Random House, 1986)

Fables by Arnold Lobel (Harper & Row, 1980)

Squids Will Be Squids by Jon Scieszka (Viking, 1998)

Should There Be Zoos? by Tony Stead (Mondo, 2002)

Web Site for Downloadable Lists of Mentor Texts:

http://www.readinglady.com/mosaic/index.htm

Nonfiction Texts Written for Kids (Magazines)

ZooNooz

Zillions

Ranger Rick

Time Magazine for Kids

Sports Illustrated for Kids

Wild Outdoor World

Web Sites

Cricket Magazine at cricketmag.com

National Geographic at nationalgeographic.com

Sports Illustrated 4 Kids at sikids.com

CHAPTER 5

Differentiated Learning at the Fluency Center

"Reading fluency refers to the ability of readers to read quickly, effortlessly, and efficiently with good, meaningful expression. It means much more than mere accuracy in reading." (Rasinski, 2003)

The center activities in this chapter provide students with practice that goes beyond the fluency work they do in whole- and small-group instructional contexts. These differentiated activities allow each student extended time to work on specific fluency targets that will help them develop expressive, accurate reading that also demonstrates comprehension, as Rasinski describes at left. The activities incorporate four areas of fluency training:

1. Fluency with Words
2. Fluency with Phases
3. Fluency with Connected Text
4. Technology-Assisted Reading

Though all students benefit from fluency work, focused activities like the ones in this chapter especially help struggling, word-by-word readers, word-callers, and readers who sound fluent but lack comprehension.

Struggling readers have typically spent more instructional time learning decoding skills at the word level than reading connected text, such as books or poems. Consequently, they have not had sufficient practice transferring their word-recognition skills to the connected text in order to develop fluency. Because accurate word-by-word reading typically uses all of their mental energies during a first reading, struggling readers benefit from activities that require them to do a second, third, and even fourth reading. This repeated practice familiarizes them with the words in the text so they can focus on the sound of the language and the meaning. In this way their reading becomes smoother and they continue to build comprehension skills.

Repeated readings also help word-callers—readers who are skilled at decoding but do not focus on reading words in an expressive way to show what the text means. By having them practice the same text, their mind-set changes from just getting through the reading to actually making sense of it through presenting it aloud in a meaningful, well-phrased way.

Even readers who sound fluent because they read accurately and with some expression may be "false positives." These are readers who are able to adeptly mimic the appropriate intonation, using punctuation cues, and sound as if they understand what they are reading. Like the word-callers, they too are missing the meaning of the text. To determine whether an expressive reader is truly fluent, ask the student higher-level questions about what they have read (see Chapter 4, Questioning). Fluent readers are able to make inferences and synthesize or draw conclusions about the information presented. Students who are false positives will benefit from the partner-reading discussions and the visualization activities with poetry and books.

How the Center Works

The formats for the activities at the fluency center are designed to be *multilevel* with a focus on helping students increase their rate of word recognition and improve their expression. To support students, make sure to provide center reading materials that are familiar texts at an easy level for each group of readers (students should be able to read these independent-level texts with 98–100 percent accuracy). Requirements for a written or pictorial response will also vary in complexity, according to students' needs.

At the fluency center, students follow a basic routine for all activities. They:

Differentiating the Same Activity

In some of the multi-level activities I provide tiered activities, from beginner to advanced. For most of the multi-level activities, however, all students follow the same procedures but use texts at their independent reading levels.

- locate the materials for the task (word cards, phrases, familiar reading material, or passages labeled with their reading level).
- participate in the independent, partner, or group activity following the modeled procedures.
- practice reading with accuracy and expression at a pace that "sounds like talking."

Teaching Tips for the Fluency Center

1. **Model and Demonstrate:** Read the same passage twice—once without expression and a second time with expression. Then brainstorm with your students what they noticed about your second reading, and you will find they can verbalize the components of fluency in their words ("You made it sound interesting," "Your voice went up when it was a question," "You talked like the character in the story," "You didn't keep stopping," "You read all the words right," and so on). Use student responses to create a class expectations chart that lists the characteristics of fluent reading.

2. **Provide Plenty of Student Practice:** To provide a reason (and motivation) for rereading the same text, focus on a different aspect each time you read the same passage. The first reading might be for enjoyment and meaning (comprehension), the second for locating high-frequency words and spelling patterns (accuracy and rate), the third for observing punctuation cues (intonation), the fourth for phrasing. Have students compare their first reading to the third or fourth. What was the difference? Which would they enjoy listening to more?

Students enjoy reading and responding to a technology-assisted reading activity at the center.

Fluency With Words

Overview of Activities: Fluency With Words				
Topic	**Activity**	**Level**	**Page**	**Repro**
Fluency with Words	• Word Reading Relay • Partner Rime Race	M M	138 139	141 141

"In her research, Ehri demonstrates that, in addition to recognizing sight words, repeated encounters with words allow readers to store patterns in their heads" (Cooper, Chard, & Kiger, 2006).

Students need to learn to read words accurately first, and then to read them automatically, without hesitation. You may have students who read words accurately, but slowly, stumbling through the text or "calling" words one by one. Struggling readers often require extensive practice in recognizing irregular sight words before they are able to store and retrieve a complete image of the word in their visual and phonological memory. When students have repeated practice reading words that contain a specific vowel pattern such as -*ake*, they are able to store these letter patterns and use these familiar word parts to decode new words. This is often referred to as "the analogy strategy."

The game and timed formats in this section are designed to provide activities that focus on increasing both the accuracy and rate with which students recognize sight words and commonly occurring vowel patterns or rimes (see Chapter 6 for more information on rimes and high-frequency words).

Teaching Tip

• During small-group instruction, add to a group word bank new sight words and words with vowel patterns that cause students to hesitate during reading. When the teaching point for the lesson includes word recognition practice, take a couple of minutes before reading to review sight words and words representing common vowel patterns. Hold up the word cards in random sequence (shuffle the deck each time) and cue students to respond together. Include multiple copies of the same words for repeated exposure and read through the words together two or three times, noting the increased rate at which students read these words. You may wish to time the group and record their "score" on a whiteboard as a visual motivation. Use these same word cards to model and practice the game formats for the Word Reading Relay and Partner Rime Race activities at the center.

To create a group or individual word bank, write sight words on index cards (or use commercial sight word cards) and store them in an index card holder labeled for the group or student.

• Demonstrate how to read lists of words in columns using a chart of words containing the rimes or vowel patterns that you are teaching during shared reading (see Activity #2). Begin with two columns of words, each of which includes words with the same pattern (for example, first column: *day*, *may*, *say*; second column: *main*, *rain*, *train*). Then present columns listing words that follow a different pattern, but have the same vowel (for example, *mice*, *light*, *tide*) so that the students have to attend closely to identify when the pattern changes. Finally, present words containing a different vowel within each column (for example, *main*, *light*, *hope*) to encourage even closer visual analysis.

- Invite students to come up and use various pointers to guide the class in reading the words on the chart.

- For a small-group mini-lesson on fluency with words, present a list of sight words or words containing useful patterns taken directly from the text you are about to read. Have students read the word list several times together before they read the new passage. Point to the words in random order after the first reading to increase students' focus. Then have students locate words from the list within the text.

Activities

Multilevel

Activity 1
Word Reading Relay

Purpose: Students will increase their accuracy and speed in reading high-frequency words.

Materials
- Word (or Phrase) Reading Speed reproducible (page 141)
- digital timer
- index cards
- student notebooks

Preparation
1. Make high-frequency word cards by printing words that students need to practice on index cards. (You may have a different set for each reading group.) Display the sets of cards at the center in a basket with the timer. Make sure to provide two copies of each word for the activity so that students will have opportunities to identify and read the word several times throughout the activity.
2. Print Yes and No on two separate index cards to be used as header cards.
3. Photocopy a Word Reading Speed form for each student.
4. Model the procedure for the relay game and for recording scores on the form.

Procedure
1. Students work in pairs or groups of three. One student sets the timer for one minute.
2. Word cards are placed in a stack facedown within easy reach of all the students.
3. Students take turns picking up a card from the stack, reading the high-frequency word and placing it under the Yes card until time is up. If one student cannot read the word, he or she passes it to the next student. If none of the students can read it, the word card is placed under the No card.

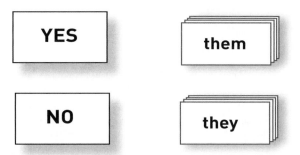

Tip

List-to-Text Reading Strategy

Have students read lists of words and then read those same words in connected text. This research-based process supports fluent word recognition and transfer to independent reading contexts. (Cooper, Chard & Kiger, 2006)

4. Students count the word cards in the Yes pile and fill in the number for the first reading on the Words (or Phrases) Reading Speed form.

5. Students repeat the process two to five times, trying to increase the number of words they read in one minute each time.

Extensions

1. Have students time how long it takes them to read all the word cards, starting the timer as they begin, and placing the word cards in the Yes and No piles as described above.

2. In their notebooks, have students make a two-column Yes and No chart. Have them record one to three words they were able to read instantly in the Yes column and any words that they didn't recognize in the No column. This provides a group record for your assessment.

Resources

An Internet search for sight-word flash cards will provide downloadable cards that can be pasted or photocopied on card stock and cut apart. Fry's sight words can be downloaded in flash-card format from www.flashcardexchange.com. Sets of sight-word cards are also readily available from teacher resource catalogues.

Technology Extension Activity

Another way to help students practice and gain automaticity with target high-frequency words (and phrases) is by using a timed PowerPoint™ display on a computer. You can create a word-by-word presentation on the screen in a timed sequence (use the Animation Scheme option) or let students reveal each word with a click of the mouse.

Activity 2
Partner Rime Race

Purpose: Students will increase their accuracy and speed in reading words.

Materials

- Word (or Phrase) Reading Speed reproducible (page 141)
- list of words containing target rimes (word families) based on current instruction or sets of commercially available word-family cards
- (optional) tracking tools for students: index card, masking card, transparent pocket chart highlighter, or Word Wildcat word-tracking tool reproducible (page 142)
- card stock and scissors
- digital timer
- colored pencil

Preparation

1. Using your list of words containing the rimes that students are studying, create a three-column form in which you present the same vowel pattern (beginner), two or three patterns with the same vowel (intermediate), or three patterns with different vowels (advanced). Copy or paste the form on card stock and display the form at the center in a basket with the timer. Alternatively, you may use word cards. (Note: students will need to count the cards each time after the timed reading unless you number them and they are kept in order. An O-ring is useful for this purpose.)

2. Photocopy a Word (or Phrase) Reading Speed form for each student.

3. Optional: Copy onto card stock the Word Wildcat word-tracking tool. Cut out the window so that it can reveal one word at a time as students slide it down the page. Provide other tracking tools as necessary, such as a transparent pocket chart highlighter.
4. Model the collaborative procedure and the use of any word-tracking tools.

Word Family Lists		
1. day	11. mail	21. name
2. game	12. play	22. trail

Procedure
1. Students take turns reading the words to each other; one student begins while the other keeps time and a record of the reading.
2. Student 1 tells student 2 when to begin reading and starts the timer.
3. Student 2 reads the words in sequence down the page or turns over the word cards in the stack one by one and reads each word. If student 2 reads all the words, he or she returns to the top of the form or to the first word card in the stack and reads the words again, until time is up. Students may use a word-tracking tool to support visual tracking, moving it down the page as they reveal and read each word.
4. While student 2 is reading, student 1 follows along on his or her copy and circles any errors or makes a tally mark for each word read incorrectly.
5. Student 1 subtracts any errors (tally marks) from the total number of words read and tells student 2 the number of words he or she has read correctly.
6. On the Word (or Phrase) Reading Speed form, student 2 records the number of words read correctly for the first reading.
7. Students repeat the process two more times, then switch roles.

Modeling Tips
Remind students to read down, not across, the lists of words. Demonstrate with word family or "rime time" charts in whole-class lessons.

Alternative Format for Independent Practice
Have students record the number of words they read in one minute or the time it took for them to read a word list or set of word cards over three consecutive readings.

Tip

Word Lists
See Resources (page 173) for lists of words and phonics charts.

Word (or Phrase) Reading Speed

Student: _____ Date: _____

1st Reading	_____ correct words/phrases per minute
2nd Reading	_____ correct words/phrases per minute
3rd Reading	_____ correct words/phrases per minute
4th Reading	_____ correct words/phrases per minute
5th Reading	_____ correct words/phrases per minute

✂ ───

Word (or Phrase) Reading Speed

Student: _____ Date: _____

1st Reading	_____ correct words/phrases per minute
2nd Reading	_____ correct words/phrases per minute
3rd Reading	_____ correct words/phrases per minute
4th Reading	_____ correct words/phrases per minute
5th Reading	_____ correct words/phrases per minute

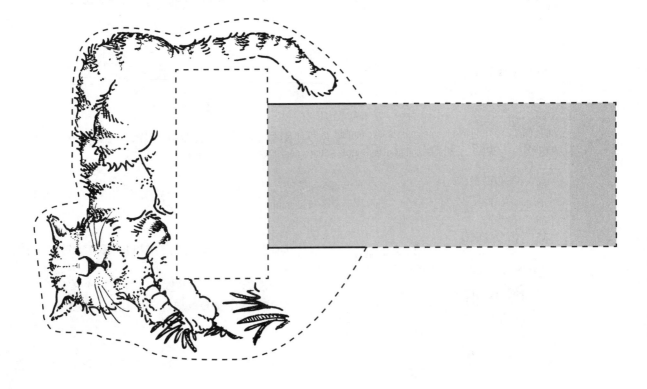

Word Wildcat (Word Tracker)

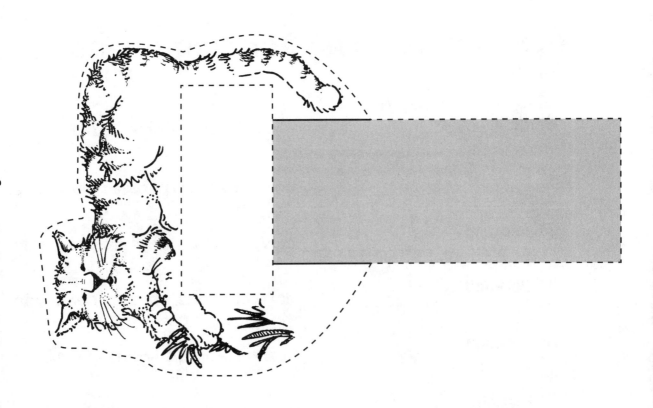

Fluency With Phrases

Overview of Activities: Fluency With Phrases				
Topic	**Activity**	**Level**	**Page**	**Repro**
Fluency With Phrases	• Fast Phrases	M	144	141
	• Froggy Phrase Slide	M	145	147–149
	• Step to the Beat	M	146	162

Struggling readers are often characterized by their laborious word-by-word reading. Yet words are rarely meant to be read in isolation; we encounter them almost always in the context of phrases and sentences. Knowing how to break a sentence into phrases, or "chunk" the text, supports comprehension; it is within these phrases that critical information is located. Students' comprehension is often negatively impacted when they break apart a phrase inappropriately, and they may lose the gist of the story. The practice activities in this section focus on reading text in phrases so that students will be able to identify these units in our language as well as increase their reading rate. With modeling and practice, students will learn to recognize the patterns in our language that signal phrase boundaries and will transfer this knowledge to their independent reading.

Teaching Tips

● Record sentences from shared-reading texts on the whiteboard and draw arcs underneath the phrases in a contrasting color. Model and have students practice "reading across these groups of words" smoothly as you scoop your hand underneath each phrase. Alternatively, on a sentence strip write a sentence containing two or more phrases. Cut the sentence into phrases and place the phrases *vertically* in a pocket chart or on the teaching table to draw attention to the phrase breaks in the text. You can use these phrases to practice the Step to the Beat activity at the center with the class or a small reading group. (Place the phrase cards in a circle around the classroom and have students walk clockwise around the room reading the phrases in sequence to reconstruct the text.)

● Present in phrases sight words students are learning, in order to put them in a meaningful context. An effective teaching practice is to combine high-frequency words you've previously taught with the ones you are currently teaching to create phrases of two to four words. Present these phrases on the overhead or chart, progressively revealing each phrase as students read them together. Record the time it took for students to read all the phrases. Challenge the class to decrease their reading time over three practice readings.

Example

Students have already practiced the words *will, all,* and *are.* You combine these words in short phrases with one of the words for this week, *they,* to develop several phrases such as those in the box at right.

> *are they all*
>
> *they are all*
>
> *will they all*
>
> *they will all*

Repeated reading of a few phrases per week not only gives students the practice they need to learn high-frequency words, but also gives them practice in reading phrases, which is key to developing fluency . . . ." (Rasinski, 2003)

- Show students that phrases tell us important information about characters, places, events, actions, or facts. Model and have students sort phrases from the text into categories "Who," "What," and "Where." (Phrases and categories can be written on sections of sentence strips or on 3- by 9-inch blank flash cards and used in a pocket chart or on a table.) This sorting and categorizing helps students look inside sentences and paragraphs to locate important information so that they can summarize the text with greater success.

Activities

Multilevel

Activity 1
Fast Phrases

Purpose: Students will increase their accuracy and speed in reading high-frequency phrases.

Materials
- Words (or Phrases) Reading Speed reproducible (page 141)
- index cards or sentence strips cut into cards
- high-frequency-word list based on your current instruction or list of sight-word phrases (see Tip)
- (optional) digital timer

Preparation
1. Select the high-frequency words you have introduced and practiced for each level of challenge.
2. Print the words on the cards or sentence strips in two- to four- word phrases. Make a duplicate copy of each phrase so students will encounter the phrase repeatedly.
3. Print "Yes" and "No" on separate index cards that will be used as category headings.
4. To support emergent learners, begin with two-word phrases, adding new high-frequency words, such as *my*, *will*, and *for* to familiar words, such as *mom*, *come*, and *me*. The phrases can even be grouped to make a short sentence or story: *my mom / will come / for me*.
5. Using a pointer or highlighter tape with a favorite big book or chart story, demonstrate how to identify phrases with high-frequency words in a familiar text. Print these phrases on a whiteboard or overhead transparency and model fluent reading of the phrases in isolation during whole class shared reading, as with this example:

   The teacher says, "Sam, don't be slow. Keep up with the group. It's time to go."

   (from *The Class Trip* by Grace Maccarone, Scholastic, 1999)

Procedure
Follow the Word Reading Relay activity procedures (page 138), replacing word cards with phrase cards.

Extensions
- **Phrase Sort:** Phrases tell us important information about characters, places, events, actions, or facts as well as how something is done or someone is feeling. Have students sort the phrases under category heading cards for *who*, *what*, *where*, and *when*.

Tip

Ready-to-Go Phrases and Short Sentences for Practice
Find an extensive list of phrases and short sentences developed from high-frequency words in Tim Rasinski's *The Fluent Reader* (Scholastic, 2003) on pages 95–99. Also see the phrase lists for Activity #2: Froggy Phrases I and II (pages 148 and 149) and the list of Resources (page 173).

Example

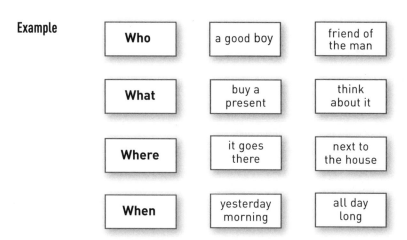

- **Generating Sentences:** Have students use the phrases to generate sentences. Ask them to complete the phrases provided in an oral or written sentence. You may also choose to provide them with phrases that make a complete sentence when combined together.

Activity 2
Froggy Phrase Slide

Purpose: Students will read with increased accuracy, phrasing, and expression.

Materials
- Froggy Phrase Slide reproducible (page 147)
- scissors
- list of high-frequency phrases based on current instruction or Froggy Phrases I and II reproducibles (pages 148–149)
- card stock
- pocket folder

Preparation
1. Make a copy of the Froggy Phrase Slide on card stock and laminate it. Cut slits along the dotted lines so that a Froggy Phrase strip can be fed through the slide. If all three levels will be using the tool during the same rotation, make a slide for each level.
2. Make copies of the Froggy Phrases pages on card stock and cut out the strips you will need (there are two at each level: beginner, intermediate, and advanced). Alternatively, make your own strips with a list of phrases generated from your students' high-frequency word lists or from stories you are reading: For each level, cut two strips of card stock 1 ½ inches wide. Print eight to ten phrases on each strip. (Follow the format of the Froggy Word Phrases strips.)
3. Color-code or otherwise label each strip so that students may choose the appropriate level. (The strips and slide tool can be stored in a pocket folder at the center.)
4. During the first rotation, set up the slide with a Froggy Phrase I strip, then remove and insert the Froggy Phrase II slip before the next center rotation or the next time you use this activity.
5. Model how to gently pull the strips through, reading one phrase at a time.

Procedure
1. Students pull the slide down to read the phrases, one by one.
2. Students may choral-read with a partner, take turns reading, or independently read the phrases.

Note: You may want to create a strip of phrases that make a complete sentence.

Activity 3
Step to the Beat

Purpose: Students will read familiar phrases with appropriate rhythm.

Materials
- Get the Beat—1, 2, 3! reproducible chart (page 162)
- copy of a familiar short text (a poem or passage from shared reading)
- sentence strips
- trimmer box or poster tube

Preparation
1. Print a familiar text in phrases or meaningful units on sentence strips. Make the print large enough to be seen from several feet away. Laminate for durability and store in a trimmer box or poster tube. Create 3 to 12 phrase strips, depending on the level of difficulty you want to offer.
2. Provide a copy of the complete familiar text at the center (poems and short texts can be printed on card stock and laminated).
3. Make a copy of the reproducible chart on card stock for use at the center.
4. Review the procedures, modeling how to read the poem fluently. Take students through the tips listed on the chart: reading with rhythm, feeling, voice, and gestures ("body").

Procedure
1. Students read the familiar text.
2. Students place the phrase strips in order on the floor, spacing them apart so that they can easily step from one to the other.
3. Students review the Get the Beat—1, 2, 3! chart.
4. Students step from phrase to phrase, reading with rhythm and expression. This is repeated three times
5. Students stop moving and read the original copy of the text a final time—smoothly and with expression.

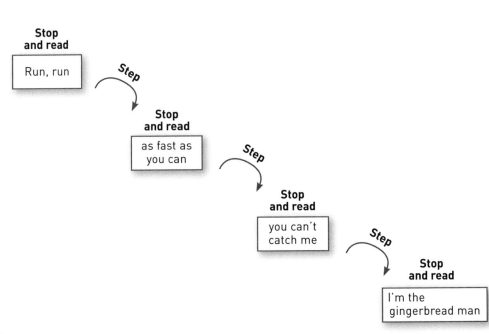

Tip

Include text with dialogue between characters, in which the tone and voice level changes from whispering to a full voice. Students can tap or stomp their feet to correspond to the degree of emphasis. (The dialogue between the quiet mouse and loud lion in the fable "The Lion and the Mouse," for example, provides such a contrast.) Circular or linear text works well for this activity, as does rhythmic poetry, such as *Noisy Poems* by Jill Bennett (Oxford, 2005).

Froggy Phrase Slide

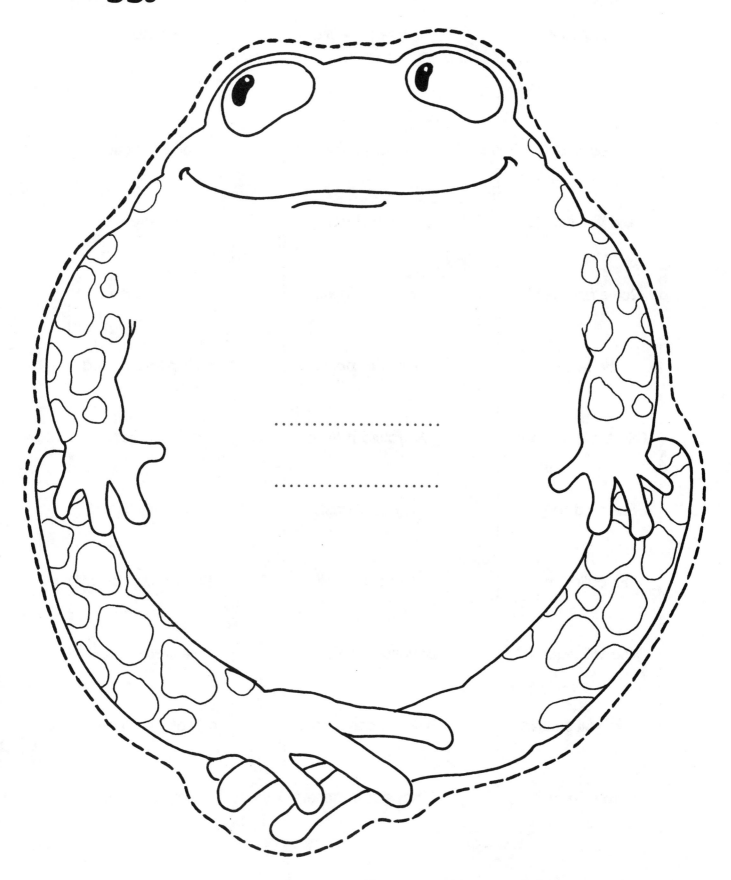

Froggy Phrases I

Beginner	Intermediate	Advanced
you and I	I know why.	a good thought
Did you see it?	a good man	along the way
Come and get it.	Write it down.	next to me
He has it.	Turn the page.	an important idea
This is a good day.	We found it here.	a few children
She said to go.	Try your best.	Talk to my friend.
He called me.	big and small	Read your book.
Who will make it?	because we should	until the end
Have you seen it?	Where does it end?	a group of friends
Want to go?	They put it there.	for example

Differentiated Literacy Centers © 2007 by Margo Southall, Scholastic Teaching Resources page 148

Froggy Phrases II

Beginner	Intermediate	Advanced
the little boy	Answer the phone.	Read every story.
then you give	Where are you?	It never happened.
with his cat	only a little	We left it here.
play with him	my new place	once upon a time
Do you know?	live and play	in the country
Here it is.	show us around	You might be right.
a long time	help me out	almost enough
Who am I?	play it again	some of the people
What did they say?	read the sentence	along the way
yes and no	You must be right.	Is it really true?

"In her research, Ehri demonstrates that, in addition to recognizing sight words, repeated encounters with words allow readers to store patterns in their heads." (Cooper, Chard, & Kiger, 2006)

Fluency With Connected Text

Overview of Activities: Fluency With Connected Text				
Topic	**Activity**	**Level**	**Page**	**Repro**
Fluency with Connected Text	• Say That Again	M*	151	160
	• Say It With Feeling	M	152	161
	• Comics and Riddles	M	153	—
	• Get the Beat	M	153	162
	• Movie in My Mind	M*	154	—
	• Tic-Tac-Poems	M	154	163
	Find a Word	M	155	—
	Highlights	M	155	—
	Build a Poem	M	155	—
	Change a Poem	M	156	—
	Class Favorites	M	156	—
	The Big Picture	M	156	—
	• Five Picks for Partner Reading	M	157	164–166
	Write and Read	M	157	—
	Buddy Reading	M	158	—
	You Choose	M	158	165
	Three Then Me	M	158	166
	Boomerang Reading	M	158	—
	• Read-a-Round	M	159	—
	• Timed Reading	I, A	159	141

* Includes specific differentiated activities for beginner, intermediate, and advanced levels. For all other multilevel activities, students follow the same activity procedure, but use texts at an independent reading level (texts they can read with 98–100 percent accuracy).

Giving struggling readers the opportunity to practice a passage until they can read it fluently helps to boost their self-image as readers. One key tool we use with connected-text activities is the use of expression during repeated readings to support much deeper comprehension of the text than an initial surface reading usually allows. Readers who practice with this emphasis not only sound more fluent, they understand the meaning behind what they're reading. For the advanced student, activities focus on expressive reading of character lines and poetry. This work develops higher-order thinking skills, as readers infer character emotions and the meaning of the figurative language used in poetry.

Teaching Tips

● Model how to use punctuation cues and make inferences about characters' emotions in order to read with appropriate intonation and expression. Take a sentence from a passage found in a big book, such as a statement a character said, write it on a sentence strip, and place the sentence strip in a pocket chart. Use the punctuation cards and the picture-cued emotion cards found in this section to cue changes in intonation and expression. Read the same sentence several times, substituting a different punctuation or emotion card each time. Invite students to practice by switching the cards in the chart and having them read the same statement with a new expression. Scaffold the activity by working with dialogue between characters in familiar fairy tales and folktales, such as the big bad wolf and the third little pig in "The Three Little Pigs." Having two characters who use very different kinds of intonation and expression sheds light on characters' motives, feelings, actions, and responses to the events in the story. You may prompt students to identify how they should read the dialogue with prompts such as, "How would the character say that?"

> "Grandmother, what big teeth you have!"

scared

- In order for oral reading fluency to engage students, there must be a motivation or purpose. Students' motivation for multiple readings of the same poem or passage is the knowledge that they will have the opportunity to perform this piece with their peers. Performance reading can include reading to a partner, a group, or the class. Organize your class into regularly scheduled oral-reading performance groups (or partnerships) and have the groups perform simultaneously to maximize your instructional time.

Activities

PRACTICE WITH PUNCTUATION AND INTONATION

Multilevel

Activity 1
Say That Again

Purpose: Students will use punctuation cues to read with expression.

Materials
- Punctuation Cards reproducible (page 160)
- card stock
- small, resealable plastic bags
- index cards or sentence strips
- (optional) cube

Preparation
1. Copy the punctuation cards on card stock and cut them apart. Place in a small plastic bag at the center.
2. Print on index cards or sentence strips character lines from familiar stories or teacher-created sentences. Place these in another plastic bag or a folder at the center. You may also wish to label and store these according to the type of punctuation they contain (sentences with exclamation marks, question marks, and so forth). For the Intermediate level variation, create sets of cards without end punctuation.
3. For the cube option, attach the punctuation cards to the six sides of the cube (simple cube-making ideas are included on page 67).
4. Show students how to read the same sentence using different punctuation prompts to guide their expression, phrasing, and intonation.

Procedure

Beginner Level

1. Students read the alphabet with punctuation. For example, *Abcde? Fghi! Jklmn. Opq? Rst? Uvw! Xyz.*
2. Students read two- or three-word phases with punctuation. For example, *My dog? You can! She will. Can we go? There it is! He said that.* (See a list of beginner-level phrases on the Froggy Phrases reproducible pages 148 and 149.)
3. Students practice reading familiar character lines cued with different punctuation marks. Then read the lines to another team member.

Intermediate Level

1. Students read the same familiar lines, using each of the punctuation cues for a different emphasis.
2. Students follow the same procedure as they read the same character line.
3. Students match up unpunctuated lines from familiar stories with the appropriate punctuation card.

Advanced Level

1. Students select a punctuation card or roll the cube and generate a sentence using that punctuation cue.
2. After reading the familiar lines, students describe the importance of these lines in the story. They may complete this activity either in writing or orally with a teammate.

Example (Intermediate/Advanced):

Teacher-created sentences	Familiar character lines
We are going on a class trip	*Grandmother, what big eyes you have*
I have homework tonight	*Little pig, little pig, let me come in*
My sister is having a party	*Somebody has been eating my porridge*

Activity 2
Say It With Feeling

Purpose: Students will use emotion cues to read with expression.

Materials

- Emotion Cards reproducible (page 161)
- card stock
- small, resealable plastic bags or cube
- index cards or sentence strips
- scissors

Preparation

1. Copy the emotion cards on card stock. You may cut the cards apart and place them in a small plastic bag or display the form as a chart at the center.
2. Print on index cards or sentence strips character lines from familiar stories or teacher-created sentences. Place in another small plastic bag or folder at the center.
3. For the cube option, attach the emotion cards to the six sides of the cube (simple cube-making ideas are included on page 67).
4. Show students how to read the same sentence using different emotion cues to guide their expression, (happy, sad, excited, angry, robot-like [no emotion], and scared).

Procedure

1. Students practice reading each character line or teacher-created sentence three or four times. Each time, before they read the line or sentence, they pick a new emotion card and use this cue to guide their expression.
2. Students read one line or sentence to a teammate using each of the emotion cues.

Activity 3
Comics and Riddles

Purpose: Students will read with increased expression.

Materials
- comic strips, jokes, and riddles at appropriate reading levels
- card stock and index cards
- scissors and glue stick

Preparation

1. Paste the comic strips on card stock and print the jokes and riddles on index cards. Laminate these materials and display them at the center.
2. Model reading the comic strips and riddles with appropriate expression.

Procedure

Students practice reading their favorite comic strip, joke, or riddle and then read it to a teammate.

Resource: *Comic-Strip Writing Prompts* by Karen Kellaher (Scholastic, 2001)

PRACTICE WITH POETRY

Multilevel

Activity 1
Get the Beat

Purpose: Students will read with rhythm and expression.

Materials
- Get the Beat—1, 2, 3! reproducible (page 162)
- familiar poems at student independent reading levels
- card stock
- folder or binder
- (optional) fluency feedback phone (PVC pipe reading tool)

Preparation

1. Copy the Get the Beat—1, 2, 3! chart on card stock laminate it and display at the center.
2. Provide familiar poems for student practice. These can be copied or printed on card stock and stored in a folder or copied and placed in a three-ring notebook at the center. (To identify the levels of challenge, copy each poem on the appropriate color of card stock or store it in a folder color-coded with a sticker.)
3. Model reading the poems with rhythm and expression.
4. If students will use fluency feedback phones, demonstrate how to use the tool to self-monitor the use of expression.

Tip

Amazing Tool for Reading Aloud
A fluency feedback phone helps students hear themselves as they read, even in soft voices. Students' voices carry through a small, curved section of PVC pipe, held like a handset to their ear. Hearing themselves loud and clear helps them adjust their rate, tone, and expression— and helps you keep noise levels down as students practice reading aloud.

Procedure

1. Students practice reading the poem using the Get the Beat—1, 2, 3! chart as a guide for their expressive reading.
2. When they have practiced reading the poem at least three times, they read it to another team member, who uses the chart criteria to give them feedback on their oral reading performance.

Activity 2
Movie in My Mind

Purpose: Students will read with increased fluency and use visualization (mental imagery) to extend their comprehension.

Materials
- familiar poems at students' independent reading levels
- magazines or advertisements
- crayons or markers
- index cards
- scissors, glue
- student notebooks

Preparation

1. (Beginner level) Create a set of sentence starters for the five senses to support students' visualization during reading: On index cards, write the simple sentence starters *I can see, I can feel, I can taste, I can hear, I can smell.* To further support students, cut out and glue to the cards pictures from magazines or advertisements that would serve as a visual cue for each sense.
2. Provide copies of familiar poems at each level for students to illustrate and practice.

Procedure

Beginner Level

1. On a copy of the poem, students draw the picture that comes into their mind as they read the poem.
2. Students label their pictures with a description of their mental images. Emergent readers and writers may use a set of sentence starters correlating to the five senses to guide them.
3. Have students practice their illustrated poems and perform them for a peer.

Intermediate and Advanced Levels

1. In their notebooks, students create a two-column format labeled "Words in the Poem / Pictures in My Mind."
2. In the first column, students record the words in the poem that helped them form mental images and in the second column, they draw or describe the pictures or images the poetry inspired.

Words in the Poem	Pictures in My Mind
Koala is the pickiest	A Koala bear picking out the best gum leaves

Activity 3
Tic-Tac Poems

Purpose: Students will read with increased fluency.

Materials
- Tic-Tac Poems reproducible (page 163)
- card stock, glue stick, index cards

- O-rings or small, resealable plastic bags
- sticky notes, highlighter pen, colored paper, stapler
- familiar poems at student independent reading levels

Preparation

1. Copy and glue the tic-tac poems board on card stock. Laminate for durability and display it at the center.
2. Provide familiar poems for students to practice reading.

Procedure

Students choose three activities to complete from the tic-tac poems board. The activities represent different levels of challenge and multiple intelligences. These activities include:

Find a Word

Preparation

Write on index cards the criteria for the types of words students must look for. Hole-punch these cue cards, and place them on an O-ring or display them in the clear plastic sleeves of a small photo album. Color-code the cards according to levels of challenge.

Procedure

On a whiteboard or in their notebooks, students record the words they discover in their poems. Examples include:
- Find words from the word wall or your word list. (Beginner)
- Find words ending with *-ate*. (Intermediate)
- Find a word that tells how something looks, feels, sounds, tastes, or smells. (Advanced)

Highlights

Preparation

List on a task card (or index cards clipped on an O-ring) the elements that students should notice as they read their poems.

Procedure

On the photocopy of the poem, students use a highlighter pen to highlight known elements, such as consonant clusters or vowel patterns they recognize (they may also use a wipe-off pen on a laminated copy of the poem).

Example: *-ag, -ip, -op, -ig*
I have a dog and his name is Rags.
He eats so much that his tummy sags.
His ears flip-flop,
And his tail wig-wags,
And when he walks,
He goes zig-zag.

Build a Poem

Preparation

Make two copies of each poem on card stock, enlarging the text so you can cut between the lines. Cut one copy of the poem into lines (easier) or phrases (more challenging). Alternatively, cut into puzzle-shaped pieces. Store both copies together in a plastic bag.

Procedure

Students reconstruct the text line by line or phrase by phrase, according to the level of challenge they need.

Change a Poem

Preparation

Provide copies of poems on card stock (or poems written on chart paper from class practice), and sticky notes or flags.

Procedure

Students write a substitution for a rhyming word, adjective or noun on the sticky note and place it directly on the text, over the original word. They read and practice their innovation, and then read it to a teammate.

Example

Pat a cake, pat a cake baker Dan.

Make me a pizza as fast as you can.

Roll it and pat it and cover it with cheese.

And deliver it to my house for dinner, please.

Class Favorites

Preparation

1. Organize copies of familiar poems into folders by level of difficulty, theme, or author.
2. Provide materials for students to make a booklet of poems, including markers and thematic cutout shapes.

Procedure

1. Students reread the photocopies of familiar poems at the center, selecting their favorites.
2. Students "publish" a booklet of poems by illustrating the selected poems. They may cut out thematic shapes or use colored paper for a cover sheet and staple together several of the poems they have illustrated.

The Big Picture

Preparation

In their notebooks, students create a two-column chart titled "This Poem is About / It Makes Me Think About."

Procedure

On the chart, students record the theme or topic of the poem in the first column and in the second column the thoughts that come to mind during and after reading.

This Poem is About . . .	It Makes Me Think About . . .
eating noodles	a noodle stretching to the sun

Say It With Feeling (see activity description, page 152)

Movie in My Mind (see activity description, page 154)

Get the Beat (see activity description, page 153)

Students can copy favorite poems from thematic collections to create their own shape books.

Multilevel

Activity 1
Five Picks for Partner Reading

Purpose: Students will read with increased fluency in a collaborative context.

Materials
- Partner Reading Chart reproducible (page 165)
- card stock
- folders
- digital timer
- Five Picks for Partner Reading reproducible (page 164)
- Fluency Feedback Form reproducible (page 166)
- Word (or Phrase) Reading Speed reproducible (page 141)
- pocket folders, small, resealable plastic bags, or bins
- multiple copies of short, familiar texts at students' independent reading levels

Preparation
1. Copy Partner Reading Chart on card stock and laminate it for durability.
2. Make copies of the Five Picks, Fluency Feedback, and Word (or Phrase) Reading Speed forms and store these in folders at the center.
3. Provide multiple copies of familiar texts for a range of reading levels at the center. These can be the dialogue from familiar stories, such as "The Three Billy Goats Gruff" and factual passages from news and science magazines for children. You may print or cut and paste these passages on card stock. (Note specific requirements for each partner activity.)
4. Model how to coach a reading buddy by using the strategy charts in the classroom, such as how to use context clues to figure out a new word or how to reread to make sense of a confusing part.

Organization Tips
1. Pair above-level readers with on-level readers and on-level readers with below-level readers.
2. Provide two copies of the same text in pocket folders, small plastic bags or bins at the center. Students may also use their individual book boxes and share the text. If students are reading the same text together use the materials of the lower performing reader. You can store these in a tub labeled "Buddy Reading."
3. (Optional) Offer matching visors or pins for buddy readers to wear to help them "get into the role."

Procedure
Students choose two or three activities to complete, marking off their selections on a copy of the Five Picks for Partner Reading form or in their notebooks. Make sure to have them write the name of their partner(s) and the titles of texts they used for each activity.

Specific directions for each activity follow.

Write and Read
1. Students work together to complete the sentence or paragraph frame. They each write their own copy in their notebooks.

Tip

Model and Practice Key Partner Social Skills
1. Look. Look at your partner.
2. Lean. Lean toward your partner.
3. Whisper. Use your "12 inch" voice.

(Feldman in Blevins, 2001)

Write-and-Read Materials

Provide sentence starters or paragraph frames from familiar, predictable texts. Omit action words, dialogue, the ending, and so on for students to fill in.

2. Students read their innovation together and practice expression and phrasing.

Example

When I was walking down the road, I saw a ___dog___ in a ___bog___ .
[animal]   [rhyming word]

Books with Repeating Sentence Patterns to Use:

(Easier)

Ten Cats Have Hats by Jean Marzollo
(Scholastic, 1994)

If You Give a Mouse a Cookie by Laura Numeroff
(Harper & Row, 1985)

If You Take a Mouse to School by Laura Numeroff
(HarperCollins 2002)

(More Challenging)

The Important Book by Mary Wise Brown
(Harper, 1949)

Things That Are Most in the World by Judi Barrett
(Atheneum, 1998)

Fortunately by Remy Charlip
(Four Winds, 1980 [1964])

(Advanced Poem-Starters)

Read a Rhyme, Write a Rhyme by Jack Prelutsky (Knopf, 2005)

Buddy Reading

1. Student 1 (the stronger reader) reads the text aloud to model fluent reading while student 2 tracks the text.
2. Student 2 reads the same text while the first student assists him or her with tricky words when needed
3. Students repeat the process to reread the same text two or three times, aiming to read it more smoothly and with more expression each time.

You Choose

1. Students read the Partner Reading Chart and choose how they will read together (choral reading, taking turns, or echo reading).
2. Students sit shoulder to shoulder to read the text. Both students support each other with any difficult words, but only if the other partner asks first.
3. Partners discuss what they have read, rereading their favorite parts to highlight the elements they like (dialogue, strong action words, and so on).

Three Then Me

1. Student 1 chooses a familiar text and reads it three times, focusing on the use of expression.
2. Student 2 listens and writes a brief evaluation on the Fluency Feedback form, noting the improvement in his or her partner's accuracy, phrasing, rate, and expression.
3. Students switch roles.

Boomerang Reading

1. Student 1 chooses a sentence and reads this aloud with expression to student 2.
2. Student 2 listens and then repeats the same sentence.
3. Students switch roles and repeat the process with a new sentence.

Tip

Partner Talk— Comprehension Link

You may want to have students record their ideas from their discussion in their notebooks. Have them draw a two-column chart titled "Favorite Parts/What We Liked." In the first column, have them write the page number and word or sentence they liked, and in the second column, describe what specific elements appealed to them.

Activity 2
Read-a-Round

Purpose: Students will read in a collaborative context with increased fluency.

Materials
- paragraphs at students' independent reading levels that can be read with expression
- card stock
- scissors
- small, resealable plastic bags

Preparation
Copy the paragraphs on card stock, laminate them, and cut them into three or four parts. Alternatively, number each paragraph in three or four parts. Store each set in a plastic bag labeled by level.

Procedure
1. The group selects a paragraph and each student chooses a numbered part to practice (readers focus on accuracy, pacing, and expression).
2. Students come together to read their parts.
3. Students may invite other students in the group to repeat (echo read) the section they have just read with the same expression they used.
4. Students switch parts and repeat the process.

Intermediate and Advanced

Activity 1
Timed Reading

Purpose: To increase the rate of reading while reading accurately and with proper expression.

Materials
- Word (or Phrase) Reading Speed reproducible (page 141)
- two copies of the same text at students' independent reading levels.
- (optional) erasable pen

Preparation
1. Provide partners with copies of the same text. You may want to laminate the copies and provide an erasable pen.
2. Show students how to take a tally of the errors and the words read correctly and record these on the Word (or Phrase) Reading Speed form.

Procedure
1. Student 1 sets the timer for one minute.
2. Student 2 reads while student 1 follows along on his or her copy and draws a line through any words read incorrectly on the page.
3. Student 2 records the number of words read correctly on the Word (or Phrase) Reading Speed form, subtracting any errors noted by student 1.
4. Student 1 rereads the passage two more times to increase his or her accuracy and speed.
5. Students reverse roles and repeat the process.

Punctuation Cards

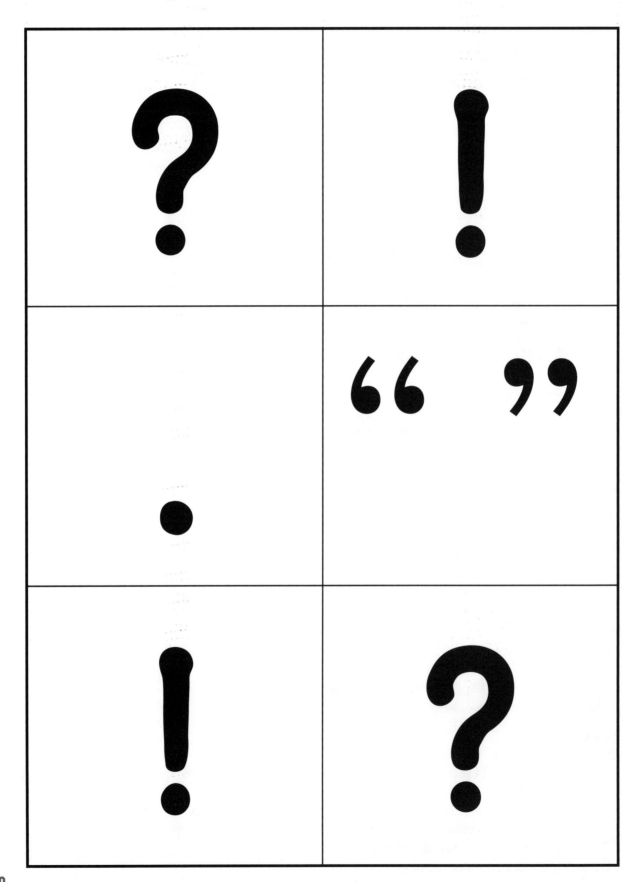

Emotion Cards

Happy

Sad

Excited

Robot-Like

Scared

Mad/Angry

Get the Beat—1, 2, 3!

1. Choose a poem.

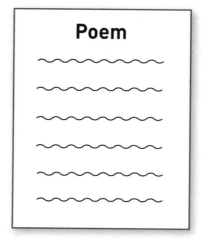

Poem

2. Read it with:

❏ Rhythm   ❏ Voice

❏ Feeling   ❏ Body

3. Read it to a friend.

162

Tic-Tac Poems

Title: _____

Author: _____

Choose three reading jobs—across, down, or diagonally.

Find a Word	Highlights	Build-a-Poem
	cat hat	
Change-a-Poem	Class Favorites	Say It With Feeling
pizza "Pat-a-~~cake~~ pizza Pat-a-~~cake~~ . . ."	★ ★ ★ ★	♥
The Big Picture	Movie in My Mind	Get the Beat

Five Picks for Partner Reading

Activity	Partner's Name	Texts We Read
Write and Read		
Buddy Reading		
You Choose		
Three Then Me		
Boomerang Reading		

Partner Reading Chart

Plan how you will read:

- Read together.

- Take turns.

- Echo read (copycat).

- Listen to your partner.

- Look at the pictures and words.

- Help your partner with tricky words when he or she asks you to.

- Share your ideas about what you read.

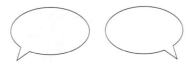

Fluency Feedback Form

Name: _____ Date: _____

Partner's name: _____

I listened to my partner read: _____.

Reading # 2: Here's how my partner's reading got better:

Circle the face that best fits the reading

- Knew more words ✓✓✓   ☺   😐   ☹
- Read more smoothly ～   ☺   😐   ☹
- Sounded like talking 💬   ☺   😐   ☹
- Used the punctuation **! ? .**   ☺   😐   ☹

Reading # 3: Here's how my partner's reading got better:

Circle the face that best fits the reading

- Knew more words ✓✓✓   ☺   😐   ☹
- Read more smoothly ～   ☺   😐   ☹
- Sounded like talking 💬   ☺   😐   ☹
- Used the punctuation **! ? .**   ☺   😐   ☹

My partner's goal is to: _____

_____

Differentiated Literacy Centers © 2007 by Margo Southall, Scholastic Teaching Resources page 166

Fluency With Technology

Overview of Activities: Fluency With Technology				
Topic	**Activity**	**Level**	**Page**	**Repro**
Fluency with Technology	• Tape-Assisted Reading	M	168	170
	• Computer Assisted Reading	M	168	—
	• Tell-a-Tape	M	169	171

Teachers can take advantage of developmentally appropriate books on disk and Web sites to support the growth of reading fluency. In addition to hearing the teacher demonstrate fluent oral reading during daily read-alouds and shared readings, a taped story or passage provides students with a second opportunity for modeled reading and multiple practice towards their individual (assessment-based) fluency goals.

For the struggling reader the technology activities can also make grade-level text and vocabulary accessible. Advanced students are able to navigate more-complex text structures with sophisticated vocabulary to challenge their higher-level thinking skills. Technology-assisted reading is not only a motivational, interactive format for all students, it provides a risk-free context that encourages independent practice.

Teaching Tips

- The technology activities can serve to build listening vocabulary and comprehension of both fiction and nonfiction text, or specifically focus on developing reading fluency, including accuracy, rate and prosody. If the purpose at the center is to develop reading fluency, then the pace of the reading needs to be aligned with the students' fluency rate. Struggling readers typically require a slower pace of reading than is available in most commercially produced taped books in order to track the text. A pace of approximately 60–70 words per minute enables them to read along rather than just listen to the text. Some commercial series provide three or four readings of the story, each one gradually increasing in the number of words per minute (for example, 10 words per minute for each reading).

Resources for Well-Paced Recorded Readings
- Read Naturally (www.readnaturally.com)
- National Reading Styles Institute (www.nrsi.com)
- Storyline Online: www.storylineonline.net offers read-alouds by popular actors from Screen Actors Guild Association (BookPALS). (Faster paced for advanced and intermediate readers.)

Short 5- to 10-minute audiotapes are available from the Web sites listed above for the Tell-a-Tape activity.

- Individual tape or CD players are preferable to multiple headsets, which can lead to time-wasting discussions and disagreements as to which student "operates the machine."

- Encourage self-monitoring and goal-setting by playing students' recorded readings during teacher-student reading conferences, and (when applicable) during small-group instruction. As you play the recording, give or elicit positive feedback so that the reader may recognize his or her progress in developing fluency skills.

"In one study from New Zealand (reported in Smith & Alley, 1997), students who read and listened repeatedly to high-interest stories on tape until they felt they could read them successfully on their own made an average gain of 2.2 years in reading achievement after participating in the study for about 27 weeks . . . . That's three times the gain expected of normally developing readers, yet these students were struggling!" (Timothy Rasinski, 2003)

Activities

Multilevel

Activity 1
Tape-Assisted Reading

Purpose: Students will read with proper phrasing, intonation and expression.

Materials
- Read-Along Chart reproducible (page 170)
- tape or CD player (preferably one for each student)
- cassette tape or CD of independent reading level text
- headphones
- copy of the text
- (optional) tracking tools (pocket-chart highlighters, pointers)

Preparation
1. Copy the Read-Along Chart on card stock and laminate for durability. Display at the center.
2. Have a student model how to operate the equipment, follow the steps in the Read- Along Chart, and store the equipment after use.

Procedure
1. Students follow the steps on the Read-Along Chart.
2. Students listen to the tape and follow along in the text. Emergent and struggling readers may use a tracking tool
3. Students stop the tape and practice reading the page or story (if it's short) on their own. They repeat this two times.
4. Students use the questions at the bottom of the chart to self-evaluate their reading. They state (either orally or in writing) how their accuracy, rate, phrasing, and use of expression improved in the second reading. Intermediate- and advanced-level students may fold a piece of paper into four and record their self-evaluation under each of the four categories (Accuracy, Rate, Phrasing, and Expression). They may also use the Fluency Feedback form on page 166.

Extension: Read Along and Respond
In their notebooks, students may write responses to their reading, using prompts from any of the comprehension activities in Chapter 4.

Activity 2
Computer-Assisted Reading

Purpose: Students will read with proper phrasing, intonation, and expression.

Materials
- computer with Internet access
- headphones

Preparation
1. Place the computer software or log onto one of the Web sites listed below.
2. Provide student headphones.

Tip

Help students record themselves independently and successfully; color-cue your tape recorder! Place sticky dots on the buttons: red on stop, green on record, and yellow on rewind.

Procedure:

1. Students read the text on the screen and respond to the software prompts. (They may also use prompts from any of the comprehension activities in Chapter 4.)

2. With students gathered around a computer to observe, model how to follow the prompts online and have a student demonstrate to the class.

Web sites for Online Reading

- Digital Text: www.icdlbooks.org offers 820 books online in nine languages.
- Student Interest Site: www.storiesfromtheweb.com offers student-written stories.

English Language Learners

Technology-assisted reading is particularly supportive of ELLs, who benefit from the opportunity to listen to a fluent English-language speaker over multiple readings. The modeling of appropriate pronunciation, phrasing, and use of new vocabulary in a meaningful context make this center a valuable source of differentiation for our ELLs.

Activity 3
Tell-a-Tape

Purpose: Students will read with proper phrasing, intonation, and expression.

Materials

- Tell-a-Tape reproducible (page 171)
- tape player
- independent-level reading text
- blank cassette audiotapes (5 minutes)

Preparation

1. Set up a tape player and blank cassette tapes at the center.
2. Make copies of the Tell-a-Tape form and store them in a folder at the center.
3. Review the procedure with students, making sure they know how to operate the tape recorder and fill in the Tell-a-Tape form.

Procedure

1. Students practice reading a page of text with expression.
2. Students place the tape in the player and push the record button to tape themselves reading.
3. Students rewind the tape and listen to their reading, checking it alongside the text. They complete the Reading #1 section of the Tell-a-Tape form and set a goal for the second reading
4. Students read and record the same selection again. Then they complete the Reading #2 section of the form, noting their improvement.

Read-Along Chart

Name: _____ Date: _____

I read _____

1. Choose a tape or CD.

2. Read along with the tape or CD.

3. Stop the recording.

4. Read the story on your own.

5. Read along with the tape or CD again.

6. Stop the recording.

7. Read it on your own.

How did your reading get better?

• I read all the words correctly

• I read groups of words together **at the park**

• I used the punctuation **! ? .**

• Speed was not too fast or slow

Differentiated Literacy Centers © 2007 by Margo Southall, Scholastic Teaching Resources page 170

Tell-a-Tape

Name: _____ Date: _____

I read _____

Reading # 1:

- Read a page.

- Tape yourself reading the page.

- Listen to the tape and check your reading with the book.

How did you do?

- It sounded like talking ☺ ☺ ☹

- I used the punctuation **! ? .** ☺ ☺ ☹

- What will you practice for reading # 2? _____

_____

Reading # 2:

- Tape yourself reading the same page.

How did your reading sound this time?

- I knew more words ✓✓✓ ☺ ☺ ☹

- I read more smoothly ～ ☺ ☺ ☹

Differentiated Literacy Centers © 2007 by Margo Southall, Scholastic Teaching Resources page 171

Fluency Menu Cards

Fluency With Words

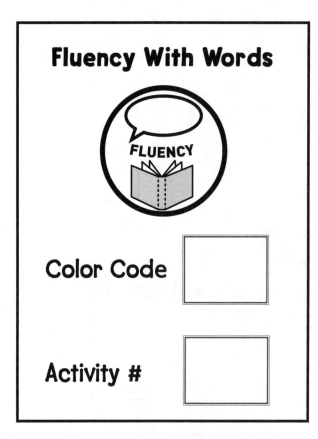

Color Code

Activity #

Fluency With Phrases

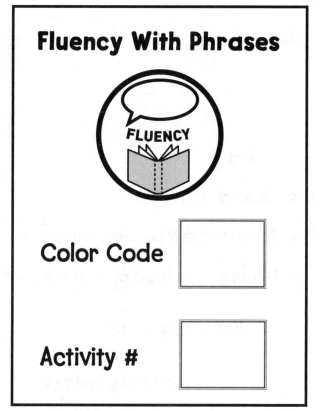

Color Code

Activity #

Fluency With Text

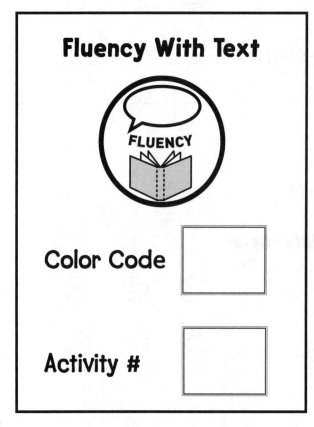

Color Code

Activity #

Fluency With Technology

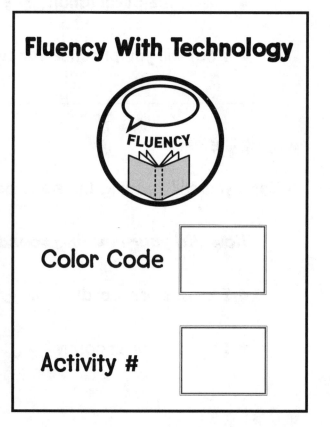

Color Code

Activity #

Differentiated Literacy Centers © 2007 by Margo Southall, Scholastic Teaching Resources page 172

Fluency With Words

A Phonics Skills Chart that outlines the progression of phonics skills from preschool to sixth grade, along with worksheets and activities is available from the Web site http://www2.scholastic.com/browse/article.jsp?id=4499

Word Family File Folder Word Walls by Mary Beth Spann (Scholastic, 2001)

Graduated word lists (speed drills) are available from www.oxtonhouse.com and www.greatleaps.com

Fluency With Phrases

Sight Word Phrases by Connie Hiebert and Sight Word Phrases Grades 1–4 both provide sets of cards, available from Crystal Springs online bookstore at www.crystalsprings.com

Fry's 300 "instant" words (1980) in *The Fluent Reader* by Timothy Rasinski (Scholastic, 2003).

Web sites for the Fry's List in phrases include: www.flashcardexchange.com

Web sites for Dolch words in phrases include: www.createdbyteachers.com; www.schoolbell.com (Dolch high-frequency words in phrases can be downloaded at no charge from these sites)

Fluency With Connected Text

Poetry Resources

TO SUPPORT DECODING:

Phonics Through Poetry by Babs Bell Hajdusiewicz (Good Year Books, 2004) (grades K–1)

More Phonics Through Poetry by Babs Bell Hajdusiewicz (Good Year Books, 2004) (grades 2–3)

Phonics Poetry: Teaching Word Families by Rasinski & Zimmerman (Allyn & Bacon, 2000)

70 Wonderful Word-Family Poems by Jennifer Wilen and Beth Handa (Scholastic, 2002)

TO SUPPORT RECOGNITION OF HIGH-FREQUENCY WORDS:

Perfect Poems for Teaching Sight Words by Deborah A. Ellermeyer and Judith Rowell (Scholastic, 2005)

TO ENGAGE READERS WITH HUMOR:

Skunks by David T. Greenberg (Little, Brown and Company, 2003)

The New Adventures of Mother Goose by Bruce Lansky (Meadowbrook Press, 1993) (innovations on familiar nursery rhymes)

Scranimals by Jack Prelutsky (Greenwillow, 2002) (multisyllabic nonsense or "Dr. Seuss" words)

Don't Go Out in Your Underwear by Babs Bell Hajdusiewicz (Dominie Press, 1997)

Antarctic Antics: A Book of Penguin Poems by Judy Sierra (Voyager Books, 2003)

Partner Reading Resources

Partner Reading: A Way to Help All Readers Grow by Allyson Daley (Scholastic, 2005)

You Read to Me, I'll Read to You: Very Short Stories to Read Together and *Very Short Fairy Tales to Read Together* by Mary Ann Hoberman (Scholastic, 2004) (text written in three colors using a supportive rhyming structure)

Boyz Rule series and Girlz Rock series (written in script format as a dialogue between two boys or girls) (Mondo Publishing, 2005)

Multilevel Readers Theater scripts are available from www.benchmarkeducation.com and www.eplaybooks.com

CHAPTER 6

Differentiated Learning at the Word Study Center

"When we say word study is developmental, we mean that the study of word features must match the level of word knowledge of the learner. Word study is not a one-size-fits-all program of instruction that begins in one place for all students within a grade level. One unique quality of word study as we describe it lies in what we believe is the critical role of differentiating instruction for different levels of word knowledge" (Bear et al, 2004).

A primary-grade classroom typically has three or four groups of students at similar levels in the areas of phonemic awareness, phonics, and vocabulary, or word study. Activity formats that are easily differentiated, such as word building and word sorting, allow *all students* to work on the same task, while providing words at an appropriate level for skill development. Activities such as these are sustainable and ongoing; you simply provide each group with a set of words matched to their needs and change the word cards or word lists at the center for each rotation.

The Word Study Center activities focus on four areas of word study:

1. Letter-Sound Relationships

2. Vowel Patterns (rimes or word families)

3. High-Frequency Words

4. Compound Words and Affixes

The Resource pages at the end of the chapter list a number of resources to support learning at the center, including books and Web sites with downloadable word sorts and word cards.

How the Center Works

At the Word Study Center, students

- locate the appropriate word cards and/or manipulatives for the task.
- participate in the independent, partner, or group activity following the modeled routines.

- practice identifying familiar phonics and spelling elements and applying these to new words.
- use multisensory formats to increase their recognition of high-frequency words.

A display of food labels and wrappers provides high-interest word-study practice.

Teaching Tips for the Word Study Center

1. **Model and Demonstrate Sorting Words:** After reading a text together, display two or three category headings for sorting the words from the text in a pocket chart or on the overhead. Read the words together and have students identify the correct category in which they belong. Encourage students to compare and contrast the features of the categories (sound, spelling, or meaning) and explain what each group of words has in common. For example, "We are going to listen for words that sound alike. Which of these words have the same sound at the end: *play, car, day?*"

2. **Provide Plenty of Student Practice:** Word sorting is a simple and very adaptable format for teaching and practicing any kind of identification and discrimination skill: identifying tricky letters, recognizing word-family patterns, distinguishing among consonants and consonant blends, and so on. You can find the basic format and procedure in the Cut and Sort activity (page 189). Game formats, such as the concentration-style game called flip-up, engage students in practice that reinforces developing word skills. (Be sure to review the rules and routines before placing the activity at the center, so that students can play independently.)

Recording Their Word Sort Work

You may require that **Beginner**-level students write two words for each category and illustrate one word for each spelling pattern. You may also ask students to use one word from each category in a sentence. **Intermediate** and **Advanced** students will be required to record more words and use at least one word from each pattern in context. In addition to this, they will be expected to reflect on what they have learned about the spelling of these words—what does each category have in common? What did they notice about these words?

Word Card and Picture Card Resources

The Resources section at the end of this chapter lists sources for picture cards and word cards that can be used in sorting activities.

Materials

Word Cards and Lists

Most activities require word cards and lists for interactive tasks like sorting. (Word cards with picture cues can help emergent and early readers, and are used in several of the beginner-level activities in this chapter.) Provide sets of word cards that meet the activity requirements (homophones, words with initial consonant blends, and so on) in resealable plastic bags or bins that are labeled by skill and level of challenge (color-code with a colored sticker). Print word lists on card stock or index cards and laminate them for durability. Label these by skill and level, too.

Sorting Mats

Generic sorting mats for the word sort activities can be simply created by dividing file folders into two or three columns. Store category heading cards and related word cards in resealable plastic bags, labeled with the word-study skill and a colored sticky dot to indicate the level of challenge. Number each bag according to the sequence that the skills are taught. For example, Sort #1 *-at, -am*; Sort #2 *-an, -ap*.

-ip	-op
hip	hop
tip	top

Word Play Book Collections

Enhance your word study center with children's books that feature the manipulation of words and explore word meanings. These books motivate students to pay attention to spelling patterns and word meanings. Consider displaying a tub of these books at the word study center. For example, provide a tub of alphabet books along with the Alphabet Recognition & Letter-Sound Relationships activities in the next section. Alongside the Vowel Pattern activities (pages 186–195) display a tub of books with rhyming text and manipulation, such as *Word Wizard* by Kathryn Falwell (see the list of Resources at the end of the chapter). Invite students to simply read and share their responses with a partner or record what they notice about the use of words in the book. (See ideas for take-out tubs on pages 76 and 77.)

Alphabet Recognition and Letter-Sound Relationships

"Adjust the pace or scope of learning according to children's needs. Don't set absolute deadlines for how much should be covered in a given time." (Blevins, 2006)

Overview of Activities: Alphabet Recognition and Letter-Sound Relationships				
Topic	**Activity**	**Level**	**Page**	**Repro**
Alphabet Recognition	• Tic-Tac-ABC Game	B	178	—
	• ABC Flip-Up	B	179	—
	• Letter Windows	B	179	—
Letter-Sound Relationships	• Picture Sorts	B	179	199
	• Picture Flip-Up	B	181	—
	• ABC Roll-and-Stack	B	181	—
	• ABC Pick Up: Initial Consonants	B	181	—
	• Word Sorts: Initial, Final, and Medial Letter Cues	B	182	199
	• Picture Sorts: Blends & Digraphs	I	183	199
	• Picture Flip-Up: Blends & Digraphs	I	183	—
	• ABC Roll-and-Stack: Blends & Digraphs	I	183	—
	• ABC Pick Up: Initial Blends & Digraphs	I	184	—
	• Word Sorts: Initial Two-Letter Blends & Digraphs	I	184	199
	• Word Sorts: Initial or Final Two-Letter Blends & Digraphs	I	184	199
	• ABC Pick Up: Three-Letter Blends	A	185	—
	• Word Sorts: Two- or Three-Letter Blends	A	185	199
	• Word Sorts: Three-Letter Blends	A	185	199

Struggling readers often have difficulty forming associations between letters and the sounds that they represent. The center activities in this section provide multiple practice opportunities for students to identify and discriminate the letters of the alphabet and recognize letter-sound relationships.

The activities in this section focus on
- single consonants and vowels
- consonant blends (or clusters of two or three consonants)
- consonant digraphs

Teaching Tips
- Notice that picture cards are sorted according to their initial, medial or final sound(s). The categories may focus on a single consonant, blend, digraph, or vowel sound. Review the names of the picture cards as some pictures can be ambiguous (for example, a picture of a dog might be mistaken for a puppy).

Many early reading
programs provide
picture-cued alphabet
cards to be used as
a memory aid during
lesson activities.
Remind students to
use these to support
their ABC activities.
An ABC word wall,
where picture-cued
word cards are dis-
played under each
letter, provides a valu-
able visual reference
(Wagstaff, 1999)

Tip

ABC Sharing Table

Ask students to bring
objects from home
whose names begin
with the letters you
are studying. Clearly
label and display these
items on a designated
table or desk in the
room. (For example,
you might create a "Bb
Table" with a bat, ball,
and bell on display,
all labeled with word
cards.)

- Emphasize sorting by sound first: Introduce sorting activities by using picture cards as the category headers, so that students will sort by sound, rather than appearance (letter-matching): "*Rake* goes under *ring* because they begin with the same sound, /r/." Avoid using pictures where the initial short vowel sound is not distinct or may result in an inaccurate pronunciation, as in the word *elephant*.

- Progress from picture sorts to picture-letter sorts: Use a letter card as the category heading for activities with letter-picture matching or sound-symbol correspondence. To demonstrate, present a picture card for students to sort. Have them state the name of the picture, the sound they hear in the target position (initial, medial, or final), and the letter they would expect to see stand for this letter: "What is the animal's name?" (*rabbit*) "What's the [beginning] sound?" (/r/) "What's the letter?" (*r*).

- Be organized and efficient when storing materials:
  - Store **picture cards** for each letter in laminated envelopes labeled "Initial," "Medial," or "Final" position to indicate the position in which the letter-sound correspondence occurs. Hole punch and fasten the envelopes together with an O-ring or use resealable plastic bags.
  - **Alphabet manipulatives** stay well organized in a variety of containers—from toolboxes or fishing tackle containers to sorting trays and small drawers, such as those used for nuts and bolts.
  - Store individual sets of **letter cards** in alphabetical order in clear plastic baseball card holders. (Plastic sheets designed for holding slides and business cards are readily available alternatives.)

Activities

ALPHABET RECOGNITION

B e g i n n e r

Activity 1
Tic-Tac-ABC Game

Purpose: Students will recognize and record letters of the alphabet.

Materials
- blank tic-tac-toe grid
- alphabet chart or letter cards
- card stock, erasable pens

Preparation
1. Display an alphabet chart or letter cards at the center.
2. Create a tic-tac-toe game board on card stock and laminate it. Provide erasable pens.
3. Have two students model how to play the game for the group.

Procedure
Partners take turns writing a letter in one of the empty boxes on the tic-tac-toe grid. They continue until one partner has filled in three spaces—horizontally, vertically, or diagonally.

Activity 2
ABC Flip Up

Purpose: Students will increase their alphabet recognition skills.

Materials
- letter cards or index cards and marker

Preparation
1. Select four to ten target letters that you have taught and students have practiced to date.
2. Gather two letter cards for each letter or make the letter card pairs by cutting the index cards in half and printing a letter on each. (You may include only lowercase letters or both uppercase and lowercase forms of each letter.)
3. Have two students model the procedure for the class.

Procedure
1. Students play a matching game. They place all the letter cards facedown on a table or mat and take turns flipping up two letter cards at a time to see whether the cards match. If the cards match, the students keep them and take another turn until there is no match. A match can consist of two cards showing the same letter or an uppercase and a lowercase form of the same letter.
2. Students tally the number of matches they've made. The player with the most matches wins the round.

Activity 3
Letter Windows

Purpose: Students will use correct formation to print letters.

Materials
- letter cards
- scissors
- copy paper
- file folder
- Velcro, paper clamp, or library pocket
- a variety of pens and pencils

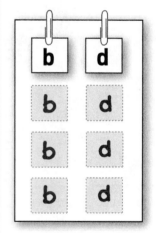

Preparation
1. Attach two letter cards at the top of the outside of the file folder with either a Velcro dot or paper clasp (for easy changes). Space them apart evenly.
2. Under the two letter cards cut out two columns of "windows," each large enough for the student to print a letter inside, approximately 1½ by 1½ inches.
3. Provide blank paper and pencils or pens at the center (vary the medium, such as gel pens, glitter pens, and markers).

Procedure
1. Students place a piece of paper inside the file folder and print the letter in the corresponding column of cutout windows. To help students distinguish between letters, such as *b* and *d*, *m* and *n*, and *p* and *q*, provide the target letter cards for repeated practice.

LETTER-SOUND RELATIONSHIPS

Activity 4
Picture Sort

Purpose: Students will match letters with the sounds they represent.

Tip

Ready-Made Picture Cards

For picture card resources, see page 222.

Materials
- picture cards for letter-sound associations you've taught
- two- or three-column sorting mat (see Sorting Mat reproducible, page 199)
- letter cards (lowercase)

Preparation
1. Determine whether students will sort words into two or three categories and which categories they will use. Picture cards can be sorted in a variety of ways. In order of difficulty:
   1. Initial sounds
   2. Final sounds
   3. Medial long-vowel sounds
   4. Medial short-vowel sounds

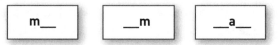

2. Provide picture cards that can be sorted into the two or three letter-sound categories you've chosen (for example, pictures that represent words beginning with *f*, *m*, and *s*). If you want students to sort pictures for final or medial sounds, prepare two or three letter cards to serve as category headings in one of two ways: a) draw a line before the letter to indicate that the sound is in the final position of the word or b) draw a line on each side of the letter to indicate that the sound is in the medial position, as shown. Place these category-heading cards along with the picture cards in resealable plastic bags.
3. Prepare the sorting mat for two or three categories.

Procedure
1. Students place a letter card at the top of each column of the sorting mat.
2. Students say the name of the picture and then place it under the letter card that represents the target letter-sound.

Differentiation Tip
To support emergent readers, have students indicate to you with their thumb in which position they hear the target sound. They point to the left for an initial sound, straight up for a medial sound, and to the right for a final sound. Make sure the picture cards represent the position of the sound in the word (for example, a picture of a mouse for *m_*, a hammer for *_m_*, and a picture of gum for *_m*).

Variations
- **Environmental Print Sort:** Provide environmental print logos or wrappers for category headings instead of letter cards to represent initial or final sounds. Environmental print resources can be downloaded from www.hubbardscupboard.org.

- **Sorting Pockets:** Fold a file folder in half and staple down the center to form two pockets. Clip a letter card to the outside of each pocket. Students sort picture cards inside the corresponding pocket. Change the letter cards for a new sort.

- **Mail ABC:** Provide a letter organizer or expandable file folder commonly available from discount and business supply stores. Label each divider by letters or letter groups, such as A–C , D–F. Students "mail" the word cards into the appropriate sections.

Extension
To support students' abilities to discriminate target sounds, add two or three picture cards that do not belong in any of the categories. Use an index card labeled "No Match" for students to use as a category heading for these pictures.

Activity 5
Picture Flip Up

Purpose: Students will improve letter-sound matching skills.

Materials
- picture cards or letter cards and picture cards representing the same sound

Preparation
1. Make a set of paired picture cards (or letter and picture cards) that represent letter-sound relationships you have taught and students have practiced.
2. Have two students model the procedure for the class.

Procedure
Follow procedures for ABC Flip Up (page 179). A match consists of two cards showing the same picture (same target letter-sound relationship) or one card with a letter and the other with a picture that represent the same sound.

Activity 6
ABC Roll-and-Stack

Purpose: Students will recognize letter-sound associations.

Materials
- picture cards
- marker
- index cards and/or cube
- student notebooks

Preparation
1. On each face of a cube (or on index cards if you're using a permanent cube with plastic pockets) write the target letters for practice using a permanent marker. (Simple cube-making ideas are included on page 67.)
2. Provide picture cards that represent the letter-sound correspondences for the letters you've chosen. Include no more than ten picture cards that represent two or three initial sounds.

Procedure
1. Students place the picture cards faceup in front of them.
2. Students roll the cube and search for a picture of a word beginning with the letter shown on the cube.
3. If this is played with a partner, the object is for each player to accumulate the most pictures in a stack.

Extension
Have students print in their notebooks three of the letters they rolled. Next to the letters, have students draw the picture from the cards that have matching letter-sounds.

Activity 7
ABC Pick Up: Initial Consonants

Purpose: Students will use initial letter cues to generate words.

Materials

- tongue depressors
- resealable plastic bags or bin
- (optional) student notebooks
- marker
- index cards

Preparation

1. Write the letters of the alphabet with a permanent marker on tongue depressors. Store these in a plastic bag or bin.
2. Print the words "Yes" and "No" on index cards and store these with the sticks.
3. Model the procedure for independent work and have two students demonstrate the game format (partner work).

Procedure

1. Students take a handful of sticks and scatter them on the table.
2. Students take turns picking up a stick and saying the name of the letter, the sound it represents, and a word that begins with that sound (for example, "*b*, /b/, *ball*").
3. If they can do this successfully, they add the stick to their pile. If they cannot name the letter, sound, and/or word, they pass the stick to the next student to try. (Students who are working independently can place the sticks in Yes and No piles.)

Extension

Have students record the letters they recognized under Yes and No columns in their notebooks.

Activity 8
Word Sorts: Initial, Final, and Medial Letter Cues

Purpose: Students will compare and contrast words using initial, medial and final letter cues.

Materials

- word cards or index cards and marker
- two- or three-column sorting mat (see Sorting Mat reproducible, page 199)
- letter cards (lowercase)
- (optional) student notebooks

Preparation

1. Determine whether students will sort words into two or three categories and which categories they will use. Word cards can be sorted by initial, final, and medial sounds; pairs of words that have the same letter in the initial and final position can be matched.

Example: Words sorted into three categories: initial, medial, and final /t/

Students can sort words by their medial vowels.

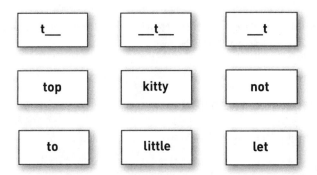

Example: Words paired by the same letter in the initial and final positions.

| g̲et | di̲g | p̲ig | ti̲p |

2. Select or create appropriately-leveled word cards that can be sorted into the two or three categories you've chosen. Select or create the two or three letter cards that will serve as category headings. Place the letter and word cards in the plastic bags.
3. Model how to sort the word cards, emphasizing the target letter sound and its position in the word: "Bat. The letter b stands for the first sound in the word bat. I will place the word bat under the letter b."

Procedure
Follow the procedure for Picture Sorts (page 179), sorting word cards instead of picture cards under the category headings.

Extension
Students record the words on a copy of the sorting mat or in their notebooks.

Intermediate

The following activities, adapted from those at the beginner level, target two-letter consonant blends and digraphs (consonant clusters) to increase the degree of challenge.

Activity 1
Picture Sorts: Consonant Blends and Digraphs

Purpose: Students will make connections between letters and the sounds they represent.

Procedure
Follow the directions for the Picture Sorts (page 179), using two or three target consonant blends or digraphs as your category heading cards.

Activity 2
Picture Flip Up: Consonant Blends and Digraphs

Purpose: Students will make connections between letters and the sounds they represent.

Procedure
Follow the directions for Picture Flip Up (page 181). Use four to eight pairs of picture cards that represent words with different consonant blends or digraphs. Or, pair the picture cards with cards showing the consonant blends or digraphs.

Activity 3
ABC Roll-and-Stack: Consonant Blends and Digraphs

Purpose: Students will make connections between letters and the sounds they represent.

Procedure
Follow the directions for ABC Roll-and-Stack (page 181). Write target consonant blends or digraphs on the sides of the cube. Students match picture cards to the consonant blend or digraph they have rolled.

Tip

Ready-Made Word Cards
For word card resources, see page 222.

Extension

In their notebooks, have students make six-boxes—one for each face of the cube. In each box, have them write the consonant blend or digraph shown on the cube and record the words represented by the picture cards that fit in that category.

Example

bl_	cl_	fl_
black	clip	flag
gl_	**pl_**	**sl_**
glass	plus	sled

Activity 4
ABC Pick Up: Initial Blends and Digraphs

Purpose: Students will use initial consonant blends and digraphs to generate words.

Procedure

Follow the directions for ABC Pick Up: Single Consonants (page 181). Write target initial consonant blends and digraphs on the tongue depressors.

Activity 5
Word Sorts: Initial Two-Letter Blends and Digraphs

Purpose: Students will compare words with single initial consonants to words in which the consonant is part of a two- or three-letter consonant blend or digraph.

Procedure

Follow the directions for Word Sorts: Initial, Final, and Medial Letter Cues (page 182). Make several category heading cards (select a consonant and one or two blends or digraphs that begin with the consonant). In this way, students can discriminate between words that begin with single consonants and those that share the initial consonant but begin with a two-letter blend or digraph. Possible sorts include:

b and *bl, br*	*c* and *cl, cr, ch*	*d* and *dr*
f and *fl, fr*	*g* and *gl, gr*	*p* and *pl, pr*
s and *sc, sl, sn, sp, st, sw, sh*	*t* and *tr, th*	*w* and *wh*

Activity 6
Word Sorts: Initial or Final Two-Letter Blends and Digraphs

Purpose: Students will compare and contrast words using initial or final two- and three-letter consonant clusters (blends and digraphs).

Procedure
Follow the directions for the word sort above, this time making category headings of either initial or final two-letter blends or digraphs that share the same initial consonant.

Extension
Have students record the words on a two- or three-column chart or in their notebooks.

sl_	sm_	sn_
slip	smell	snack

Advanced

The following activities, adapted from the beginner and intermediate levels, target three-letter consonant clusters, such as *spl* in *splash*.

Activity 1
ABC Pick Up: Three-Letter Blends

Purpose: Students will use initial consonant blends to generate words.

Procedure
Follow the directions for ABC Pick Up: Initial Consonants (page 181). Write target three-letter consonant blends on the tongue depressors.

Activity 2
Word Sorts: Two- or Three-Letter Blends

Purpose: Students will compare and contrast words using two or three letter consonant blends and digraphs.

Procedure
Follow the directions for Word Sorts: Final, and Medial Letter Cues (page 182). Make category headings that begin with two- and three-letter blends that begin with the same letter such as *sp-, spl-, spr-*, and *str-*.

Activity 3
Word Sorts: Three-Letter Blends

Purpose: Students will compare and contrast words using three-letter consonant blends.

Procedure
Follow the directions for the activity above, making category headings with target three-letter blends, such as *scr, spr,* and *str.*

"The best differentiator between good and poor readers is repeatedly found to be their knowledge of spelling patterns and their proficiency with spelling-sound translations."
(Marilyn Adams, 1990)

Vowel Patterns

	Overview of Activities: Vowel Patterns			
Topic	**Activity**	**Level**	**Page**	**Repro**
Vowel Patterns (Rimes)	• Magic Mat	M	187	196
	• Wrapper Rimes	M	188	197
	• Story Rimes	M	189	—
	• Cut and Sort	M	189	198, 199, 200
	• Find a Rime	M	190	—
	• Word Games	M	191	—
	• House of Rimes	B	192	201
	• Flap Book	B	193	—
	• Tic-Tac-Rime #1	B	193	196, 199, 202
	• Build Big Words	I	193	196
	• Big Word Puzzles	I	194	—
	• Tic-Tac-Rime #2	I, A	195	203
	• What's the Same?	A	195	—

Learning to recognize common vowel patterns in new words is critical for developing accuracy and fluency in reading. As opposed to sounding out letters in isolation, recognizing clusters of letters in rimes is a much more efficient way to read. The study of rimes also makes instructional sense because rimes generate so many words. Researcher Edward Fry (1998) found that knowing just 38 rimes generated 654 one-syllable words and many multisyllabic words as well.

Readers who are tuned in to patterns like these can employ the analogy strategy—they break down unfamiliar words into parts and apply the patterns they recognize to figure out the word. This strategy is useful in decoding and spelling single-syllable words (*cat*: *-at* pattern), and even more importantly, multisyllabic words (*habitat*: *-ab* and *-at* patterns). Not surprisingly, struggling readers often demonstrate difficulty transferring their knowledge of spelling patterns to new words and new reading contexts (Gunning, 2002). The activities that follow provide ample practice with vowel pattern identification for struggling students and students who need decoding practice.

Teaching Tips

- Familiarize yourself with the key terms related to vowel patterns before you work with these activities:
  ○ *Onset*—the consonant, consonant blend, or digraph that comes before the rime in a syllable (*c* in *call*).
  ○ *Rime*—the vowel and letters that follow it in a syllable (*-all* in *call*). A rime always sounds the same, and must also be spelled the same way, as in the words *hair* and *fair*. A rime is different from a word family in that words in the same family may sound the same or rhyme, but may have different spellings, as with the words *meet* and *meat*.

- Many teachers are concerned, for good reason, that students will simply focus on the visual cues during word sorts, attending to the pictures and/or letters rather than reading the words to form both a sound and pattern association. Partner sorting and game activities address this concern. Including words that are exceptions in the sort and adding an "out of sorts" or "misfits" category heading helps to keep students focused on both visually scanning words for familiar patterns and assigning a pronunciation.

Differentiated Learning in Action

- **Making Word Sorts More Challenging:** Word sorts can be made more challenging by asking students to sort them by categories such as parts of speech (noun, verb, adjective), words that sound the same yet have different spellings (homophones, such as *plain* and *plane*), and words that can be pronounced in more than one way (homographs, such as *wind* and *live*).

- **Big Words, Simple Patterns:** Struggling readers in second and third grade may be less self-conscious working with simpler patterns alongside their peers if you provide multisyllabic words containing these less challenging rimes, such as *sunset* and *habitat*. The list of decodable multisyllabic words (page 220) has words with short and long vowel patterns correlated to common rimes, as well as more challenging vowel combinations for Intermediate and Advanced readers to apply their rime recognition and syllabication skills.

- **Food Phonics and Brand Names:** Ask students to bring in labels and wrappers containing the spelling traits you are studying. Highlight the vowel pattern with a marker and invite students to share other words that contain the same pattern students have heard or seen. Labels may be used as category headings on these brainstorming or "rime time" charts. Refer to these during reading and writing activities throughout the day.

Activities

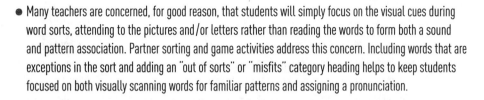

M u l t i l e v e l

These activities are appropriate for students at beginner, intermediate, and advanced levels of word study. It is the complexity of the vowel pattern that will vary for each group of students. Select the appropriate patterns as you prepare the word cards, manipulatives, and word lists for the following activities.

Activity 1
Magic Mat

Purpose: Students will generate new words by changing the onset or rime.

Materials
- Magic Mat reproducible (page 196)
- card stock
- tactile letters (magnetic, foam, tiles, cards) or index cards and marker
- two or three word cards with rimes highlighted (one word card for each target rime)
- resealable plastic bags
- student notebooks

Tip

Word Sorts

"Word sorts help students get repeated exposure to words as well as give them an opportunity to look at words closely from a certain perspective. This is especially important for struggling readers who don't do this automatically and need opportunities to think about words." (Strickland, 2005)

Preparation:
1. Copy the Magic Mat form on card stock and laminate it.
2. To create your own word-building manipulatives, instead of using tactile letters and word cards, cut index cards in half. Print onsets on one half and target rimes on the other. Include letters or onset and rime cards that will build three to five words for each rime.
3. Store the word cards and letters (or your onset and rime cards) together in plastic bags at the center.
4. To support emergent readers, provide a list of words that contain the target rimes for students to build with their card set.
5. Introduce the activity with a book that illustrates the process of combining letters to form new words, such as *Word Wizard* by Kathryn Falwell or *Show and Tell Disaster* by Mike Reiss. Model the procedure combining tactile letters or letter cards with the rimes shown on the word cards.

Procedure
1. Students place the letters in the area at the top of the mat.
2. Students choose a word card (or rime card) and generate two to four words containing the rime by pulling down the letters they need from the top of the mat and building the words inside the frame at the bottom of the mat.
3. Students copy in their notebooks the words they have made.

Modeling and Guided Practice Tip
Model how to pronounce the onset and the rime separately at first and then blend the two units together to say the word as you run your finger underneath. Have the students repeat this with you. Demonstrate changing the onset to form a new word in the same manner and have students join in by pronouncing each part and then blending the parts to say the whole word. Provide practice with onset and rime cards in which partners or small groups of students combine the cards to build words.

Activity 2
Wrapper Rimes

Purpose: Students will identify rimes in environmental print.

Materials
- Wrapper Rimes reproducible (page 197)
- wrappers or labels illustrating target rimes
- highlighter tape
- resealable plastic bags

Preparation
1. Make copies of Wrapper Rimes reproducible and store the copies in a file folder.
2. Print the target rimes on index cards (see the previous activity).
3. Paste labels and wrappers on card stock. Store these along with the rime cards in plastic bags. Alternatively, laminate the wrappers so that students can use an erasable highlighter pen to mark the rime.
4. Model the procedure.

Procedure
1. Students find familiar rimes in the food word or brand name shown on the wrapper. They highlight these with highlighter tape.
2. Students draw the wrapper in the left column of the Wrapper Rimes form. Next, they write the word they found on the wrapper and highlight or underline the rime it contains.

Tip

Wrapper Words

Sources for labels and wrappers include cereal boxes, labels from canned goods, and candy wrappers. (See also Picture Sort resources on page 222.)

Management Tips

1. List the rimes you are studying in your newsletters to parents and caregivers, and request that students bring in labels and wrappers with words containing these rimes for the center.
2. Cut highlighter tape into short pieces and attach them along the edge of a strip of laminated card stock. Students take a piece of tape to highlight a word. When they've recorded the word on their form, they return the tape to the holder.

Activity 3
Story Rimes

Purpose: Students will use rimes to write a story or poem.

Materials
- list of words containing target rimes or a rime-time chart (see Teaching Tip, page 187)
- writing paper

Preparation
1. Introduce the activity with a literature springboard (see Resources for the Fluency Center, page 173).
2. List words containing the rimes you are studying from a familiar read-aloud or shared-reading text. Students will use these words to create their own text.
3. Model how to generate a story or poem using these words. Include student names where possible.

> Use the words from *Sheep in a Jeep* by Nancy Shaw to write your own story.
>
> | sheep | jeep | steep |

Procedure
Students read the list of words and any literature models at the center. They use the words and ideas or text structure to compose a story or poem.

Activity 4
Cut and Sort

Purpose: Students will compare and contrast words by their vowel patterns.

Materials:
- Cut and Sort reproducible (page 198)
- Sorting Mat reproducible (page 199)
- (optional) What's My Sort? reproducible (page 200)
- scissors
- student notebooks

Tip

See the list of Resources at the end of the chapter for Web sites and books with reproducible word sorts.

Preparation

1. Select two or three words containing target rimes for category headings or use several rimes or vowel patterns alone as headings. Write them in the boxes at the top of the Cut and Sort form. Underline the rimes (-*ame* or *name*).
2. In the boxes on the Cut and Sort form, write in random order 12 words containing the target rimes. Copy the completed form on card stock and cut apart the word cards and category headings (alternatively, students can cut them out). Store them in a labeled plastic bag.
3. Copy the Sorting Mat on card stock and store it with the rest of the materials.
4. Model how to sort the words on the overhead or in a pocket chart. (For example, "Stay. This word ends with the same pattern as *day* . . . Who can help me put this one in the right category?")

Procedure

1. Students put the category headers (with rimes underlined) across the top of the sorting mat.
2. Students examine each word in the set to find the pattern. They sort the word cards under each category heading on the sorting mat.
3. If this is a partner activity, students may take turns reading through the cards together before beginning the sort.
4. In their notebooks, beginner-level students will write and illustrate one or two words for each pattern. Students at intermediate and advanced levels write the words in columns in their notebooks (you may also make copies of the Sorting Mat that they can write on). Below each column, students write a sentence stating what the words in each category have in common. For example: "All of these words have the -*ame* rime."

Variation: Student-Selected Open Sort

Create an open sort in which students identify commonalities among a set of related words. For this open-ended sort, provide word cards that can be grouped together in a number of possible ways—by spellings, sounds, or meanings (concepts from your class literature units, social studies, and science, such as *character traits/actions* and *mammals/birds/fish*). Model the procedure by presenting a list of words from a shared text. Ask students, "How are some of these words alike?" Have pairs of students name two or three categories and discuss which words might fit in those categories. Let students work together to fill in a What's My Sort? form.

Activity 5
Find a Rime

Purpose: Students will recognize familiar rimes within words.

Materials

- reading materials (stories or poems) containing target rimes
- index cards and marker, O-ring
- writing paper or student notebook

Preparation

1. Select reading materials at students' independent reading levels. Provide index cards with the rimes students are to seek and find in the selected material. (These cards may be displayed on an O-ring.)
2. Introduce the activity with a book that illustrates the process of locating familiar parts in words, such as *There's an Ant in Anthony* by Bernard Most (Morrow 1980).

Tip

Poems With Rimes
For ideas, see the poetry section in Resources for the Fluency Center, page 173.

Procedure

1. Students locate the target rimes in classmates' and story characters' names, books, poems, charts, dictionaries, and the word wall, and record them on the form. This may be a cooperative activity in which individual students add words to a classroom chart.

2. Students can hunt for target patterns in collaboration with one or more partners. When working in a small-group context, one student is the recorder, one the reader, another the checker, and so forth. Emphasize that every group member is expected to contribute at least one word to the chart: have students put their initials next to the words they find (Ganske, 2000).

Word Games

Roll-a-Rime

Purpose: Generate words using familiar rimes.

Procedure

Write a set of six target rimes on the faces of a cube. Students roll the cube and must come up with a word that contains the rime shown. You may require that they record the words or simply share them orally with a partner. Challenge intermediate-level students by having them roll the cube with rimes and a die. They must generate the number of words indicated on the die. Advanced-level students can generate a multisyllabic word that contains one or more target rimes.

Rime Rummy

Purpose: Build words by matching onsets and rimes.

Procedure

- Prepare the game cards by writing the initial consonant or consonants on a set of 20 cards (include blends and digraphs for intermediate- and advanced-level students) and the rimes or vowel patterns on another 20 cards. Students put the onset cards in one pile and rime cards in the other.

- Students take turns picking up one card from each pile to see if they can make a real word. If they can, they keep those cards. If not, then the rime cards go into a common bank.

- When the bank gets too "full" (10–12 cards), these cards are placed at the bottom of the pile to be recycled with the existing rime cards. The goal is for each player to accumulate as many words as possible.

Rime Flip Up   *concentration*

Purpose: Recognize familiar rimes within words.

Procedure

- Follow the directions for ABC Flip Up (page 179). If specific vowel patterns are the focus, include word cards that follow the pattern and list these rimes on a card that accompanies the game. Otherwise include a variety of words that contain rimes students have been working on and let the grouping process be open-ended; students look for a common spelling pattern in each word pair they turn over.
- Students use a deck of 16–25 word cards. Students place them facedown in a four-by-four or five-by-five array.

- This can be an independent or group activity. If it is a group activity, each player turns over two cards on his or her turn. If the player can identify a common pattern and the rest of the group agrees, then the player collects these cards and takes another turn. When no more matches can be made, the game is over.

Partner Sort

Purpose: Discriminate rimes within words (auditory to print).

Procedure

- Follow directions for Word Sorts: Initial, Final, and Medial Letter Clues (page 182).
- Partners spread the category heading cards in front of them and place the word cards in a nearby stack for sorting.
- Student 1 holds all the word cards and reads them aloud one at a time without showing student 2.
- Student 2, without looking at the word, indicates the correct category by touching and saying the category card. Student 1 places the word card under the category card. Then they reverse roles, so that both students have an opportunity to read and categorize the words (Bear et al, 2004).

Beginner

Activity 1
House of Rimes

Purpose: Students will recognize and record familiar rimes.

Materials

- House of Rimes reproducible (page 201)
- writing paper, pencils
- (optional) library pocket and rime cards (e.g., *-ake*)

Adding a library card pocket to the form on page 201 allows you to exchange rime cards frequently.

Preparation

1. On a copy of the House of Rimes form, print the target rime or vowel pattern in the door shape on the form. Alternatively, laminate the form and attach a library pocket to the door. Insert a rime card in the pocket for students to use as a reference. This allows for easy changes.
2. Make copies of the House of Rimes form, fold the copies in half to make booklets, and store them in a folder at the center.
3. Model the procedure. Point out to students that the door illustrates the concept that if you know one rime, it opens the door to many new words that you can read and write.

Procedure

Students read the rime in the door on the outside of the booklet. Inside the booklet they print three words that contain the rime and illustrate one of the words.

Activity 2
Flap Book

Purpose: Students will recognize and record familiar rimes.

Materials

- copy paper
- index cards, O-ring or resealable plastic bags
- folder
- scissors

Preparation

1. Fold a sheet of paper in half lengthwise and make two cuts on the top half to create a cover with three flaps (see the Retelling Flap Book activity and format on pages 108 and 113). You may make the books or guide students through the steps to make their own. Store the books in a folder at the center.
2. Print target rimes on index cards and store the cards on an O-ring or in plastic bags.
3. Model the procedure for using the flap book.

Procedure

1. Students select three rime cards. On each flap, students copy one of the rimes.
2. Under each of the flaps, students write and/or draw a word containing that rime.

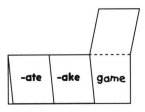

Activity 3
Tic-Tac-Rime #1

Purpose: Students will recognize and record familiar rimes.

Materials
- Tic-Tac-Rime #1 reproducible (page 202)
- word cards with rimes highlighted
- Sorting Mat reproducible (page 199)
- sticky notes
- card stock
- flap books
- Magic Mat reproducible (page 196)
- student notebooks

Preparation

1. Copy the Tic-Tac-Rime form on card stock and laminate it.
2. Set out materials for each of the activities presented on the tic-tac-toe grid.
3. Model each activity. You may want to review the procedures for Magic Mat (page 187). Activities in the top row and Story Rimes can be recorded in students' notebooks. The sticky notes from the last activity can be collected here, too.

Procedure:

Students choose three activities on the Tic-Tac-Rime board to complete.

Intermediate

Activity 1
Build Big Words

Purpose: Students will make multisyllabic words using onsets and rimes.

Materials
- Magic Mat reproducible (page 196)
- letter cards or tactile letters (magnetic, foam, tiles, cards)
- list of Decodable Multisyllabic Words (page 220)
- card stock
- student notebooks

Preparation

1. Copy the Magic Mat form on card stock and laminate it.
2. Store the letter cards or tactile letters in bags or divided trays at the center.

3. On card stock or index cards, print multisyllabic words containing target rimes and display them at the center.
4. Model the procedure.

Procedure
1. Students select a multisyllable word from the list or cards.
2. Students place the letters they need to build the word in the area at the top of the Magic Mat.
3. Students pull down the letters and build the word inside the frame at the bottom of the mat. This is repeated for three to five words.
4. Students copy in their notebooks the words they've made.
5. Challenge students to generate and record two or three more multisyllabic words with the same vowel patterns.

Activity 2
Big Word Puzzles

Purpose: Students will make multisyllabic words using onsets and rimes.

Materials
- index cards, marker, scissors
- list of Decodable Multisyllabic Words (page 220)
- resealable plastic bags
- student notebooks

Preparation
1. Print multisyllabic words containing target rimes from the list on index cards. Cut the cards apart into onsets and rimes and display these at the center, placing several cut-up words in a plastic bag for students to reconstruct. Note that some words consist of a sequence of rimes (see example below), while others also include onsets for each syllable, as in *midnight*. The number of words in each bag will depend on the level of challenge you can offer these students. To provide additional support, you may also provide a card with the answers for self-checking.

2. Model the procedure.

Procedure
1. Students lay out all the cards on the table and build a multisyllabic word using the onset and rime cards.
2. Students check their answers and then record in their notebooks the words they have created.

Activity 3
Tic-Tac-Rime #2 (INTERMEDIATE/ADVANCED)

Purpose: Students will recognize and record familiar rimes.

Materials
- Tic-Tac-Rime form #2 (page 203)
- materials for each of the activities listed
- card stock

Preparation
1. Copy the Tic-Tac-Rime #2 form on card stock and laminate it.
2. Model each activity listed.

Procedure
Students choose three activities on the Tic-Tac-Rime board to complete.

Advanced

Activity 1
What's the Same?

Purpose: Students find similarities among words by comparing spellings, sounds, and meanings.

Materials
● 1 6–25 word cards representing different consonant blends, digraphs and rimes; common meaning associations

Preparation
1. Provide word cards that can be grouped together in various ways, such as sound, spelling and meaning.
2. Model the procedure by presenting a pair of words and asking students to identify how they are similar in some way (see Cut and Sort, Open Sort Variation, page 190).

Procedure
This word-pairing activity follows the ABC Flip Up format (page 179). Students turn over two cards and identify how the words are alike in some way. (The words do not have to contain the same spelling pattern.) This generalization can be based on either letter-sound associations (blends and digraphs), spelling patterns (rimes), or meaning (content-area words, such as weather terms).

Extension
Have students complete a Venn diagram of what is the same and what is different about one of these word pairs.

Magic Mat

A ★ B • C ★ A • B ★ C • A ★ B C • A

B   B

C   C

A   A

B   B

C   C

A   A

★ B • C ★ A • B ★ C • A ★ B C • B ★

Wrapper Rimes

Name: _____ Date: _____

Draw the Wrapper ✏️	Write + Highlight 💡

197

Cut and Sort

Category 1	Category 2	Category 3

Sorting Mat

Category 1	Category 2	Category 3

Differentiated Literacy Centers © 2007 by Margo Southall, Scholastic Teaching Resources page 199

What's My Sort?

Name: _____ Date: _____

- Find words that are the same in some way.

- Sort the words into two or three groups.

Word List

_____   _____

_____   _____

_____   _____

_____   _____

_____   _____

_____   _____

_____   _____

Categories

1._____

2._____

3._____

Group 1	Group 2	Group 3

Differentiated Literacy Centers © 2007 by Margo Southall, Scholastic Teaching Resources page 200

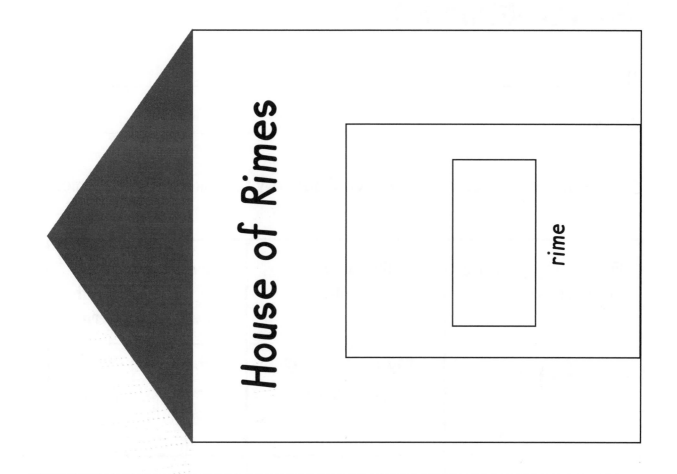

House of Rimes

rime

Tic-Tac-Rime #1

Title: _____

Author: _____

Choose three jobs across, down, or diagonally to make a Tic-Tac-Rime.

Find _____ words with the same pattern. **tip**	Use a word in a sentence. My dog is **big** and yellow.	Draw pictures of _____ words with the same pattern. frog · log
Make a three-rime flip flap book. -ate · -ake · game	You choose! ☺	Write a story or poem using words that have the same rime.
Build three words on the Magic Mat. a ★ b c	Do a word sort. -ip / -op · hip tip / hop top	Write three words on sticky notes and put them in ABC order. A · B · C

Tic-Tac-Rime #2

Title: _____

Author: _____

Choose three jobs across, down, or diagonally to make a Tic-Tac-Rime.

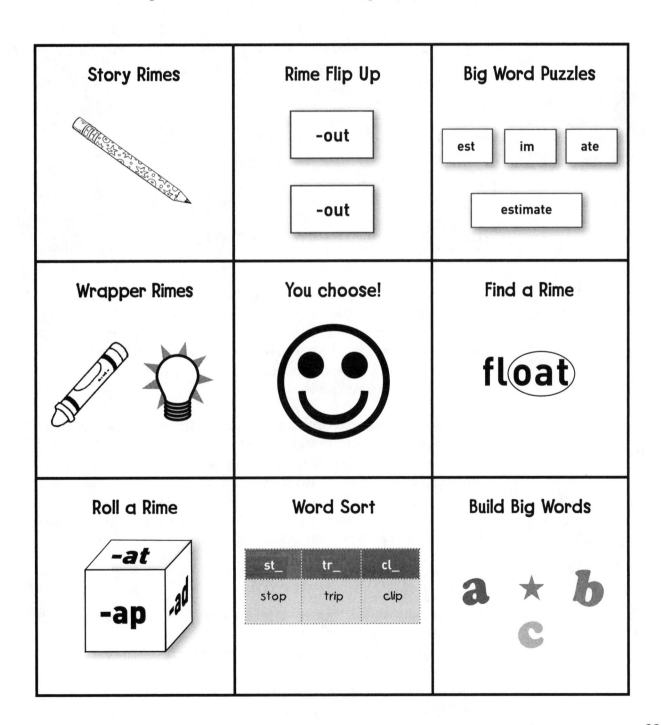

Story Rimes	Rime Flip Up	Big Word Puzzles
Wrapper Rimes	You choose!	Find a Rime
Roll a Rime	Word Sort	Build Big Words

"High-frequency words, commonly known as sight words, are the 200 or so most frequently occurring words in printed English. Unfortunately, many of the most frequently occurring words . . . lack a distinctive appearance and so are easily confused with other words (will, with, what); and may have a spelling that gives little or no clue to their pronunciation (one, of)." (Gunning, 2002)

High-Frequency Words

Overview of Activities: High-Frequency Words				
Topic	**Activity**	**Level**	**Page**	**Repro**
Vowel Patterns (Rimes)	• Mix and Fix	M	205	210
	• Flip-Up Sight Words	M	206	—
	• Partner Tic-Tac-Read	M	206	—
	• Sight-Word Hunt	M	206	—
	• Word Windows	B	206	—
	• Rebus Sentence	B	207	—
	• Sight-Word Sorts #1	B	207	199, 199
	• Tic-Tac Look-and-Say #1	B	207	198, 199, 210, 211
	• Tic-Tac Look-and-Say #2	I, A	207	—
	• Word Pyramids	I, A	207	—
	• Sight-Word Sorts #2	I	209	198, 199
	• Sight-Word Sorts #3	A	209	198, 199
	• Sound Alikes: Homophone Flip Up	A	209	—

Students do not learn high-frequency words with irregular spellings (*does, some*), as easily or quickly as ones with regular spellings (*that, did*). You may find that some of your students require repeated practice over an extensive period of time before they master both reading and spelling of these words. Particularly challenging are high-frequency words beginning with *t* and *w, wh-* and *th-* such as *then, them, than; there* and *their; want* and *went*; and *were* and *where*. These share common letters and are easily confused if students do not attend very carefully to the letters in sequence.

The beginner-level activities in this section help students who need to practice shorter, more regular sight words with supportive initial and final letter-sound relationships, such as the *w* and *s* in *was*. Regular, multisyllabic words and irregular sight words serve as appropriate challenges for intermediate-level students. Most challenging for our students are the complex vowels and silent consonants in the medial position in words such as *people* and *thought*. These tricky spellings are an appropriate focus for advanced students, who may be able to read these words in connected text and in isolation, but confuse the letter sequences or omit letters in their spellings. To vary the level of challenge, designate specific practice word cards for groups and individuals.

Teaching Tips

● Model sorting sight words at different levels of difficulty. For example, your class might be working at these distinct levels of challenge:

1. Mastering automaticity with initial consonants or consonant clusters (blend, digraph). Example: words that begin with *t* and *th, w* and *wh*.

2. Noticing patterns. Example: *-ould* words, *-ere* words.

3. Distinguishing sounds. Example: Homophones such as *their* and *there, where* and *wear*.

Tip

It is important that students have the opportunity to develop automaticity in recognizing these words both in isolation and in context. (Rasinski, 2003)

- Play games like "Guess the Missing Letter" that develop visual memory skills using a game show format. Cover one or two letters in the sight word and invite students to identify the missing letters. (Omit the initial and final sounds first. Omit the trickier medial spellings when students are ready for a challenge.)

- Support kinesthetic learning with activities that involve clapping or tapping the letters of words in sequence. You can also support the students' auditory memories by making available sight word songs from commercial CD's and reading programs or creating your own chants and rhymes with high-frequency words. Tap into students' visual learning capacity by offering word walls and word banks, including:

  ○ **Class Word Wall:** A high-frequency word wall organized by initial letters provides a visual reference for students to self-check these words, which require mastery.

  ○ **Individual Word Walls:** For younger students these "walls" may be file folders filled with library pockets and labeled *A–Z* (hint: combine *x, y, z*). Index cards are used to record and file each word in the library pockets of the appropriate folder. Older students may use a file folder that has been divided into 13 sections labeled alphabetically, in which they record the words they study.

  ○ **Reading Group Word Banks:** Word cards with the high-frequency target words from small-group instruction are stored in a resealable plastic bag that is labeled for that group. Students locate the words in poems and books at the center and then reread them in context (see Sight-Word Hunt, page 206).

  ○ **Personal Word Banks:** Students may create their own word bank by printing each target word on one side of a card (e.g., *for*) and on the other side including the word in a phrase or sentence (e.g., *pizza for me*). These can be stored in a file folder with library pockets labeled *A-Z* or on an O-ring.

Activities

Activity 1
Mix and Fix

Purpose: Students will use manipulatives to represent the correct letter sequence of high-frequency words.

Materials
- Mix and Fix reproducible (page 210)
- resealable plastic bags
- tactile letters
- high-frequency word cards
- card stock
- student notebooks

Preparation
1. Copy the Mix and Fix form on card stock and laminate it.
2. Provide word cards in a plastic bag at the center, labeled for specific groups of students.
3. Model how to build the word on the Mix and Fix form, then check the letter sequence by chanting each letter on the word card in sequence as you touch the corresponding manipulative.
4. Have a student or pair of students come up and fix letters you have mixed up.

Procedure
1. Students place the word cards in the first column of the form.
2. Students build the word with manipulative letters in the second column.

3. Next they turn over the word card, mix up the letters, and rebuild the word three times. Students turn the card back over and check their spelling.

4. Students record the word in their notebooks.

Extension

For an additional challenge, include an "oddball" letter that does not belong and see whether students can discriminate the letters they need from among the array.

Activity 2
Flip-Up Sight Words

Purpose: Students will read high-frequency words with accuracy.

Procedure

Follow the directions for Rime Flip Up (page 191). Use high-frequency word cards or picture cards at the appropriate level for each group.

Activity 3
Partner Tic-Tac-Read

Purpose: Students will spell high-frequency words with accuracy.

Procedure

Follow the directions for Tic-Tac-ABC Game (page 178). Partners take turns filling in a blank tic-tac-toe grid with sight words from their word banks or word cards you have provided. Students may use different-colored erasable pens to support visual discrimination.

Activity 4
Sight-Word Hunt

Purpose: Students will locate high-frequency words within connected text.

Procedure

Follow the directions for Find-a-Rime (page 190). Provide sight-word cards for students to seek and find in the reading materials at the center (books and poems). (Store the cards in a resealable bag or on an O-ring.) Students record the word and the number of times they found it (it occurred in text) during their sight-word hunt (e.g., *said*—3, *was*—5, *they*—2).

Beginner

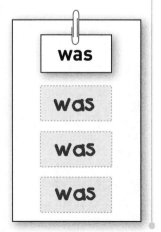

Activity 1
Word Windows

Purpose: Students will spell high-frequency words with accuracy.

Procedure

Follow the directions for Letter Windows (page 179), cutting in a single column down the front of the folder four rectangular "windows" approximately 1½ by 4 inches.

● Attach a high-frequency word card to the top of the folder with either a Velcro dot, paper clamp, or library pocket. The student places a piece of paper inside the folder and copies the word through the four folder windows using a variety of mediums, such as gel pens or markers.

Activity 2
Rebus Sentence

Purpose: Students will construct a complete sentence using high-frequency words and pictures.

Materials
- picture cards
- high-frequency word cards or index cards and a marker
- resealable plastic bags
- student notebooks

Preparation
1. Create the picture cards by pasting on card stock high-interest pictures of people, animals, places, and actions found in magazines and advertisements. Cut the picture cards apart and store them in plastic bags at the center.
2. Provide high-frequency word cards at the center that will form sentences when combined with the picture cards. Alternatively, print high-frequency words on index cards.
3. Model arranging the picture and word cards to form a complete sentence.

Procedure
1. Students select words and pictures to build a rebus sentence.
2. In their notebooks, students can record their words in rebus format and read aloud their sentences.

My		was	on	the	

Activity 3
Sight-Word Sorts #1

Purpose: Students will compare and contrast sight words based on their letter sequence.

Procedure
Follow the directions for Cut and Sort (page 189). Select the high-frequency words students need to practice with and fill in the category headings and word card spaces on the Cut and Sort form (page 198). Categories for sorting the word cards include:
- Beginning Letters: Same and Different (*me*, *my*—same; *can*, *will*—different)
- Final Letters: Same and Different (*was*, *his*—same; *was*, *saw*—different)
- Number of Letters in a Word: Two, Three, and Four (*get*—three; *tree*—four)

Activity 4
Tic-Tac-Look-and-Say #1

Purpose: Students will read high-frequency words with accuracy.

Materials
- Tic-Tac-Look-and-Say #1 reproducible (page 211)
- Materials for each of the activities listed

Preparation

1. Copy the Tic-Tac-Look-and-Say #1 form on card stock and laminate it.
2. Model each activity listed.

Procedure

Students choose three activities from the grid to complete.

Intermediate and Advanced

Activity 1
Tic-Tac Look-and-Say #2

Purpose: Students will read high frequency words with accuracy.

Materials

- Tic-Tac-Look-and-Say #2 reproducible (page 212)
- card stock
- materials for each of the activities listed, including a set of sight words at the appropriate level.

Preparation

1. Copy the Tic-Tac-Look-and-Say #2 form on card stock and laminate it.
2. Model each activity listed.

Procedure

Students choose three activities from the grid to complete. Note:

- Rainbow Words requires the students to print the target words using different-colored pencils.
- For the Word Wall or Word Bank activity, students build and write words from the word wall or group or individual word bank.
- Card Games allows students to choose from commercial sight-word card games in your collection. These include variations on bingo, go fish, and lotto.

Activity 2
Word Pyramids

Purpose: Students will record high frequency words with accuracy.

Materials

- high-frequency word cards or index cards and marker
- resealable plastic bags
- writing paper, pencils

p
pe
peo
peop
peopl
people

Preparation

1. Display the high-frequency word cards you've selected for this group in a plastic bag at the center. Alternatively, print selected high-frequency words on index cards and display these cards in the same way.
2. Model the procedure of building a word from its initial letter by cumulatively printing the letters of the word on each line until the word is complete, creating a pyramid shape.

Procedure

1. Students choose a card and read the high-frequency word.

2. Students write the word cumulatively starting at the top of the page with the first letter of the word and adding a new letter at the end of each line. The last step is to draw a triangle around the word.

Activity 3
Sight-Word Sorts #2

Purpose: Students will compare and contrast sight words based on their letter sequence.

Procedure
Follow the directions for Cut and Sort (page 189). Categories for high-frequency word sorts at the intermediate level include:

- Single Initial Consonant and Consonant Blends or Digraphs (*t* and *th*; *w* and *wh*)
- Final Letters: Same and Different (*where* and *there*; *them* and *then*)
- Medial Vowels: Same and Different (*come* and *done*; *went* and *want*)
- Patterns (*-ould*, *-ere*, *-en*)

Advanced

Activity 1
Sight-Word Sorts #3

Purpose: Students will compare and contrast sight words based on their letter sequence.

Procedure
Follow the directions for Cut and Sort (page 189). Categories for high-frequency word sorts at the advanced level include:

Categories include:
- Silent Consonants: Yes and No (*could*, *laugh*—Yes; *sleep*, *best*—No)
- Silent Vowels: Yes and No (*does*—Yes; *well*—No)
- Same Sound (Homophones): Spelling 1 and Spelling 2 (*to*—spelling 1, *two*—spelling 2)

Activity 2
Sound Alikes: Homophone Flip Up

Purpose: Students will read high-frequency homophones with accuracy.

Materials
- high-frequency word cards with homophones at students' level of challenge or index cards and marker

Preparation
Provide or create pairs of high-frequency homophone word cards such as the examples at right.

Procedure:
Follow the directions for Rime Flip Up (page 191). The object is to make a pair by turning over two cards with words that sound the same (matching homophones).

High-Frequency Homophones
eight/ate
made/maid
cent/sent
weak/week
two/too
threw/through
know/no
read/red
their/there
would/wood
for/four
buy/by
where/wear

Mix and Fix

Name: _____

Date: _____

Letters	Word Cards
i a d s	said

Tic-Tac Look-and-Say #1

Title: _____

Author: _____

Choose three jobs across, down, or diagonally to make a Tic-Tac-Look-and-Say.

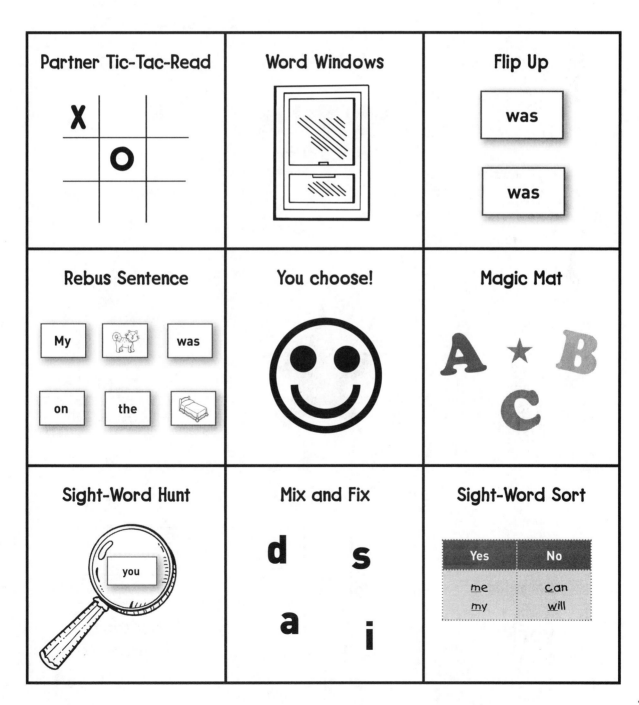

Partner Tic-Tac-Read	Word Windows	Flip Up
Rebus Sentence	You choose!	Magic Mat
Sight-Word Hunt	Mix and Fix	Sight-Word Sort

Tic-Tac Look-and-Say #2

Title: _____

Author: _____

Choose three jobs across, down, or diagonally to make a Tic-Tac-Look-and-Say.

Sight-Word Hunt	Sight-Word Sort	Mix and Fix
you	w_ / wh_ — were, went / where, when	s e d o
Word Pyramids	**You choose!**	**Card Game**
p, pe, peo, peop, peopl, people	★	Go Fish!
Rainbow Words	**Tic-Tac-Read**	**Flip Up**
work, work, work	X O	because, because

Differentiated Literacy Centers © 2007 by Margo Southall, Scholastic Teaching Resources page 212

Compounds and Affixes

Overview of Activities: Compounds and Affixes				
Topic	**Activity**	**Level**	**Page**	**Repro**
Compounds and Affixes	• Add-a-Word	B	214	217
	• Compound Flip Up	B	214	217
	• Suffix Flip Up	I	214	218
	• Prefix Flip Up	I	215	218
	• Beginnings and Endings	A	215	218
	• Prefix and Suffix Flip Book	A	216	218

As the complexity of text increases, students require word-analysis strategies to decode and comprehend multisyllabic words. Learning to identify familiar words within compound words and meaningful parts of words, such as affixes, assists in both decoding and comprehension. To support struggling readers at the multisyllabic level, build on the sight words they already know with simple compound words. More advanced students can use affixes and base words to create new words, extending both their reading and spelling vocabularies.

Teaching Tips

- Compound Words: When modeling how to find smaller words within compounds, remind students to look for words with more than two letters; otherwise they may identify parts of words that are not helpful, such as the *so* in *some*. You can help students avoid this confusion by asking them to check if each of the little words can stand on its own, such as *class* and *room* in *classroom*. The most frequently occurring compounds begin with the words *some*, *any*, and *every*. Brainstorm compound words that begin with familiar sight words.

some	**every**
someone	everyone

- Prefixes: Focus on the meanings of the prefixes, noting that many have more than one meaning. Remind students to be careful of clusters that look like prefixes but aren't, such as *un* in *uncle*. To determine whether a group of letters is a prefix, students can remove them from the word and check whether a root or base word remains. Students should use context cues as well as examine the parts of a word to verify a word's meaning.

"un" (prefix)	**"un" (part of a word)**
undo	uncle

Materials

- Color-code prefix, base word, and suffix cards for the word-building activities to support visual learners. Possible colors include green for the prefix, blue or yellow for the base word, and orange or pink for the suffix. Store these in alphabetical order in an index card holder for making quick changes at the word study center.

"Good readers effectively search for different sources of visual information in print and shift rapidly to using chunking or patterns of information because it is more efficient. There are several natural breaks in words: syllables, inflection breaks, prefixes and suffixes, and rime breaks. Children use these breaks to assist them." (Askew, 1999)

Activities

Beginner

Activity 1
Add-a-Word

Purpose: Students will make compound words from short, high-frequency words.

Materials
- Compound Word Cards reproducible (page 217)
- student notebooks
- card stock

Preparation
1. Copy the Compound Word Cards form on card stock and cut the cards apart. Store them in a plastic bag at the center.
2. Model combining the Compound Word Cards to form new words.

Procedure
1. Students select two word cards and place them together to form a compound word.
2. Students write in their notebooks the compound words they make.
3. If students are working as partners, one can read the smaller words and then build the compound word while the other records it. Then they can switch.

Activity 2
Compound Flip Up

Purpose: Students will combine high-frequency words to build compound words.

Procedure
Follow the directions for Picture Flip Up (page 181). Copy the Compound Word Cards on card stock and cut them apart (or create your own set of compound word cards by selecting a set of words and writing each half of a compound word on separate index cards). On each turn, students will turn over two cards and see whether they can make a compound word. If they can, they keep the pair. The object is to collect as many compound words as possible.

Intermediate

Activity 1
Suffix Flip Up

Purpose: Students will add suffixes to build new words.

Materials
- Suffix Cards reproducible (page 218)
- card stock, scissors
- index cards
- resealable plastic bags

Preparation:
1. Copy the Suffix Cards on card stock and cut them apart.
2. Cut the index cards in half. Print the base words below on the index card halves. Store both sets of cards in separate plastic bags.

Procedure

Follow the directions for Picture Flip Up (page 181). On each turn, a student turns over two cards—a base word (index card) and a suffix (colored card). If the cards make a true word, the student keeps the cards. The object is to collect as many words as possible.

Base Words

re_	dis_	mis_	un_	non_
play	cover	spell	do	sense
build	agree	match	able	fiction
turn	like	place	afraid	living
read	count	behave	happy	stop

_ly	_ful	_less	_ness	_est
quiet	forget	spot	dark	quick
glad	color	help	weak	safe
loud	care	power	sick	fast
brave	use	price	fair	high

Activity 2
Prefix Flip Up

Purpose: Students will add prefixes to build new words.

Procedure

Follow the directions for Suffix Flip Up, substituting Prefix Cards (page 218) for Suffix Cards.

Guided Practice Tip

Discuss the meanings of common prefixes, including these:

re—again	**un**—not, opposite of	**dis**—not, opposite of	**mis**—wrongly
in—not	**non**—not	**fore**—before	**pre**—before
over—too much			

Advanced

Activity 1
Beginnings and Endings

Purpose: Students will substitute suffixes and/or prefixes to form new words.

Materials
- Prefix and Suffix Cards reproducible (page 218)
- index cards and marker
- resealable plastic bags
- list of base words (above)
- card stock
- student notebooks

Preparation

1. Copy the prefix and suffix cards on different colors of card stock and cut the cards apart. Store the cards in plastic bags at the center. Cut the index cards in half. Print the list of base words on the index card halves.
2. Model how to combine the prefix, base-word, and suffix cards to form new words.

Procedure

1. Students select three cards at a time: a prefix, a base word, and a suffix. They arrange the cards in front of them to see whether they have made a word.
2. Students write in their notebooks the multisyllabic words they make.
3. If students are working as partners, one student can read the affixes and base word and then build the multisyllabic word while the other records it. Then they can switch.

Extension

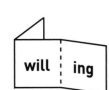

Students make a "flip-strip" of one of their multisyllabic words to practice reading. They print the word on a 9- by 3-inch flash card or strip of card stock, and bend back the prefix and suffix to read the base word (Johns & Lenski, 2000). Then they unfold the prefix and read the longer word. Finally they unfold the suffix and read the full word. (For example, *will . . . unwill . . . unwilling*).

Activity 2
Prefix and Suffix Flip Book

Purpose: Students will build multisyllabic words.

Materials
- Prefix and Suffix Cards reproducible (page 218)
- card stock, scissors
- three-ring binder
- list of base words (page 215)
- index cards and marker
- student notebooks

Preparation

1. Copy the prefix and suffix cards on different colors of card stock and cut them apart. Cut index cards in half and write the base words you've selected on them.
2. Hole punch the cards and place them in a three-ring binder placed in "landscape" position. Place the cards in sequence to form a word: prefix, base word, suffix.
3. Model the procedure of mixing and matching the three word parts to form multisyllabic words.

Procedure

1. Students mix and match the affixes and base words to create new words by flipping a new card on the ring.
2. In their notebooks, students record the words they build.

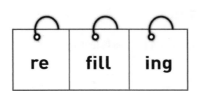

Compound Word Cards

every	any	some	thing
where	one	body	day
way	sun	light	back
shine	yard	ball	foot
base	down	day	town

Prefix Cards

un	re	dis	in
fore	mis	non	over

Suffix Cards

ly	est	ful	ness
less	s	ing	ed

Differentiated Literacy Centers © 2007 by Margo Southall, Scholastic Teaching Resources page 218

Word Study Menu Cards

Alphabet Recognition and Letter-Sound Relationships

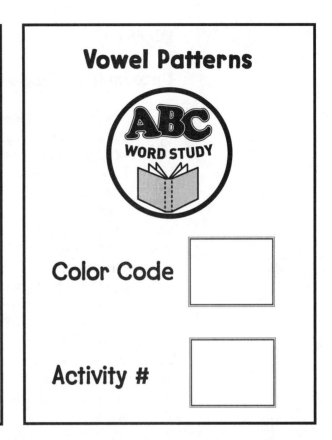

Color Code

Activity #

Vowel Patterns

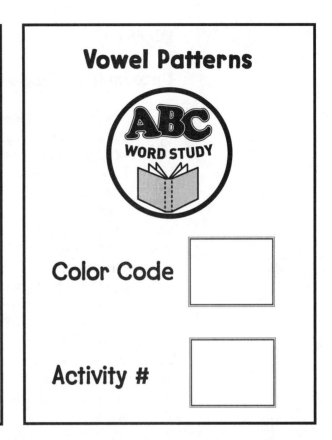

Color Code

Activity #

High-Frequency Words

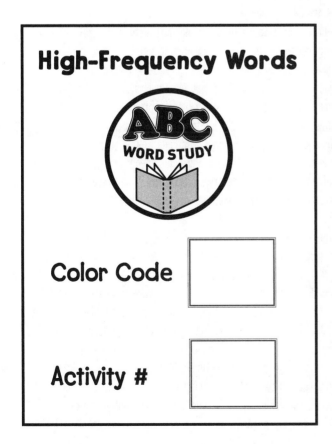

Color Code

Activity #

Compounds and Affixes

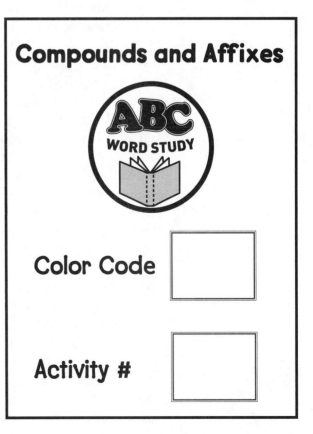

Color Code

Activity #

Word Lists

Decodable Multisyllabic Words

ack: backpack, backtrack, crackerjack, fullback, haystack, icepack, jacket, racetrack, racket, soundtrack, thumbtack, unpack, paperback, quarterback

ail: airmail, cottontail, detail, fingernail, pigtail, railroad, retail, thumbnail, toenail

ain: contain, explain, maintain, obtain, remain, restrain, tearstain, unchain, refrain

ake: awake, cupcake, earthquake, fruitcake, handshake, keepsake, mistake, pancake, remake, snowflake, rattlesnake

ale: exhale, female, inhale, nightingale, tattletale, telltale, wholesale

ame: became, inflame, nickname, surname, overcame

an: anaconda, ancestor, animal, Batman, began, branches, Canada, Japan, dishpan, outran, pecan, planning, suntan, handyman, Superman

and: bandstand, candle, command, cowhand, demand, expand, grandstand, headband, landed, landscape, quicksand, standard

ank: banker, blanket, cranking, Frankenstein, gangplank, outrank, thanking

ar: apartment, partner, calendar, charming, farmer, starting, depart, popular, separate

ap: catnap, chapter, gingersnap, handicap, happen, hubcap, kidnap, kneecap, mishap, mousetrap, napkin, overlap, rapid, unhappy, unwrap

ash: bashful, cashew, dashboard, eyelash, flashlight, smashing, stashing, whiplash

at: acrobat, aristocrat, Atlantic, attic, chatter, chitchat, clatter, matter, doormat, habitat, muskrat, scatter, scratching, tomcat, thermostat, wildcat, wombat

ate: calculate, playmate, celebrate, separate, cooperate, classmate, debate, decorate, donate, create, estimate, frustrate, graduate, hibernate, illustrate, imitate, inflate

aw: awesome, awful, drawing, clawing, crawling, jigsaw, outlaw, strawberry, yawning

ay: away, birthday, crayon, daytime, display, faraway, everyday, okay, subway, Norway, holiday, weekday, today, railway, repay, stingray, highway, halfway, hallway, player

eat: backseat, defeat, heartbeat, mistreat, overeat, repeat, retreat, treated, upbeat

ell: Cinderella, doorbell, eggshell, farewell, unwell, misspell, umbrella, yellow, nutshell

en: attend, defend, depend, intend, pretend, unbend, overspend, comprehend, blender

er: reverse, universe, conversation, insert, dessert, deserve, unnerve, conserve, preserve

est: biggest, contest, digest, forest, hardest, harvest, interest, investigate, protest, restful, suggest, yesterday, destination

ice: advice, device, entice, overpriced, sacrifice

ick: candlestick, chicken, chopstick, drumstick, homesick, lipstick, nickel, pickle, pumpernickel, sticky, thicken, toothpick, yardstick, pinprick, tricky, quickly

ide: beside, bedside, collide, confide, decide, divide, fireside, outside, worldwide, reside

ight: alright, delight, headlight, highlight, midnight, moonlight, overnight, sunlight, tonight

ill: caterpillar, uphill, gorilla, refill, thrilling, windmill, vanilla, windowsill, chinchilla, anthill

in: begin, cabinet, dinner, finished, inside, invite, unpin, winner, window, splinter, hairpin

ine: combine, porcupine, valentine, sunshine, airline, grapevine, hemline, sideline

ing: bingo, finger, flamingo, plaything, singing, single, something, stinging, everything

ink: blinking, crinkle, rethink, shrinking, sinking, sprinkler, stinky, thinking, twinkle, wrinkle

ip: catnip, dipping, unzip, tripping, dripping, fingertip, friendship, penmanship, spaceship

it:	admit, kitten, permit, unfit, benefit, transmit, outfit, omit, misfit, armpit, moonlit, outwit
ock:	padlock, pocket, unlock, stockings, livestock, sunblock, ticktock, locker, roadblock
op:	operate, raindrop, hilltop, gumdrop, nonstop, tiptop, treetop, lollipop, bellhop
or:	acorn, afford, forget, fortune, record, report, resort, support, transport, uniform, morning, popcorn, important, indoor, normal, order, thunderstorm, perform
ore:	adore, before, carnivore, drugstore, explore, ignore, ashore, anymore, restore
ot:	cannot, forgot, jackpot, robot, teapot, snapshot, slingshot, grasshopper, flowerpot
uck:	bucket, chuckle, lucky, potluck, thunderstruck, unlucky, woodchuck, buckle
ug:	bedbug, juggle, ladybug, litterbug, snuggle, unplug, earplug, fireplug, struggle
ump:	bumpy, dumping, grumpy, jumping, pumpkin, lumpy
unk:	sunken, chunky, spunky, chipmunk, junky, pre-shrunk, bunker

Compound Words

Two Syllable (Easy):

suntan, sunglasses, sunlight, cannot, without, hilltop, cupcake, batman, jellyfish, bedroom, pigtail, play-pen, catnap, catfish, backstop, bedbug, pancake, backpack, haystack, uphill, lipstick, chopstick, pigtail

Two Syllable (Challenging):

someone, something, somewhere, snowball, doorbell, airport, homemade, teammate, cowboy, butterfly, eyesight, staircase, seashore, roadblock, railway, cookbook, campground, highway, sunlight, outside, rainfall, fireplace, homework, nighttime, playground, cornfield, housework, raincoat, seafood, sidewalk, notebook, driveway, hallway, wildlife

Three Syllable:

anyone, anything, anybody, anytime, anywhere, everybody, everything, everyone, everywhere, grandmother, grandfather, afternoon, however, whenever, butterfly, overcome, overlook, underground, litterbug, thunderstruck

Resources for the Word Study Center

Word Building

Word Family Wheels by Liza Charlesworth (Scholastic, 2000)

Systematic, Sequential Phonics They Use by Patricia Cunningham (Carson-Dellosa, 2000) (word building sequence)

Easy Lessons for Teaching Word Families by Judy Lynch (Scholastic, 1999) (word building for the 37 most common rimes)

30 Wonderful Word Family Games by Joan Novelli (Scholastic, 2002)

Picture Sorts

Picture This! Picture Sorting for Alphabetics, Phonemes and Phonics by S. Nielsen-Dunn (Teaching Resource Centre, www.trcabc.com)

Word Sorts for Letter Name-Alphabetic Spellers by Johnston, Bear, Invernizzi & Templeton (Prentice Hall, 2003)

Environmental print Web site: www.hubbardscupboard.org

Word Sorts

All Sorts of Sorts (grades K-4) and All Sorts of Sorts 2 (grades 3-8), and #3 (Vocabulary) by Sheron Brown (Teaching Resource Center) (reproducible word sorts for a range of developmental levels)

Word Journeys by Kathy Ganske, (Guilford Press, 2000) (sorting activities and word lists)

Word Sorts and More: Sound, Pattern and Meaning Explorations (K-3) by Kathy Ganske, (Guilford Press 2006) (reproducible picture and word sorts, word lists)

Word Sorts for Alphabetic-Letter Name Spellers by Johnston, Bear, Invernizzi & Templeton (Prentice Hall, 2003)

Words Their Way: Word Sorts for Within Word Pattern Spellers by Johnston, Bear, Invernizzi & Templeton, (Prentice Hall, 2004)

Scholastic Rhyming Dictionary by Sue Young (Scholastic, 2006) (single and multisyllabic words organized by rhyming patterns)

Helpful Web sites

Learn to Read at Starfall, www.starfall.com (online activities)

Rhymezone Rhyming Dictionary and Thesaurus, www.rhymezone.com

WordPlay, wordplay.com

Reading A-Z, readinga-z.com (activities and resources)

High-Frequency Words

Perfect Poems for Teaching Sight Words by Deborah Ellermeyer and Judith Rowell, (Scholastic, 2005)

Reading Skills Card Games: Sight Words by Liane B. Onish (Scholastic, 2004)

Sight Word Manipulatives for Reading Success by Deborah Schecter (Scholastic, 2005)

Scholastic High Frequency Word Readers

Flashcards, www.flashcardexchange.com (downloadable sight-word list in flash-card format)

Word Play Collections

Things That Are Most in the World by Judi Barrett (Atheneum, 1998) (-est, -iest suffixes)

Fortunately by Remy Charlip (Aladdin, 1993) (prefix un-)

Word Wizard by Kathryn Falwell (Clarion Books, 1998) (making new words from the same letters)

Knock, Knock! Who's There? By Tad Hills (Little Simon, 2000)

There's an Ant in Anthony by Bernard Most (Morrow, 1980) (familiar parts in multisyllabic words)

Andy (That's My Name) by Tomie de Paola (Prentice-Hall, 1973) (making new words from the same letters)

The Great Show- and-Tell Disaster by Mike Reiss (Price Stern Sloan, 2001) (making new words from the same letters)

Once There Was a Bull...(frog) by Rich Walton (Gibbs Smith, 1995) (compound words)

Professional Literature Cited

Adams, M. (1990). *Beginning to read: Thinking and learning about print.* Cambridge, MA: Massachusetts Institute of Technology.

Allington, R. (2005). *What really matters for struggling readers: Designing research-based programs.* (2nd ed.). Boston: Pearson.

Askew, B.J. (1999). "Helping Young Readers Learn How to Problem Solve Words While Reading." *Voices on Word Matters,* 143–155, Fountas & Pinnell eds. Portsmouth, NH: Heinemann.

Bear, D.R., Invernizzi, M., Templeton, S. & Johnston, F. (2004). *Words their way: Word study for phonics, vocabulary, and spelling instruction.* (3rd ed.). Upper Saddle River, New Jersey: Pearson.

Blevins, W. (2006). *Phonics from A to Z.* (2nd Ed). New York: Scholastic.

Blevins, W. (2001). *Building fluency: Lessons and strategies for reading success.* New York: Scholastic.

Boyles, N.N. (2004). *Constructing meaning through kid-friendly comprehension strategy instruction.* Gainesville, FL: Maupin House.

Caldwell, J.S. & Leslie, L. (2005). *Intervention strategies to follow informal reading assessment.* Boston: Pearson.

Cooper, J.D. Chard, D.J. & Kiger, N.D. (2006). *The struggling reader: Interventions that work.* New York: Scholastic.

Cunningham, P. (1995). *Phonics they use: Words for reading and writing.* New York: HarperCollins.

Dole, J.A. (2004). The changing role of the reading specialist in school reform. *The Reading Teacher,* 57, 462–471.

Drapeau, P. (2004). *Differentiated instruction: making it work.* New York: Scholastic.

Fox, B.J. (2000). *Word identification strategies: Phonics from a new perspective.* Upper Saddle River, NJ: Prentice-Hall.

Fountas, I.C. & Pinnell, G.S. (1996). *Guided reading: Good first teaching for all children.* Portsmouth, NH: Heinemann.

Flynt, E., & Cooter, Jr., R.B. (2005). "Improving Middle-Grade Reading in Urban Schools: The Memphis Comprehension Framework." *The Reading Teacher,* 58, 774–780.

Fry, E. (1998). "The most common phonograms." *The Reading Teacher,* 51, 620–622.

Fry, E.B. & Kress, J.E. *The reading teacher's book of lists.* (2006). (5th ed.). San Francisco: Jossey-Bass.

Ganske, K. (2000). *Word journeys: Assessment-guided phonics, spelling, and vocabulary instruction.* New York: Guilford.

Gardner, H. (1993). *Frames of mind: The theory of multiple intelligence.* NY: Basic.

Gregory, G. & Chapman, C. (2002). *Differentiated instructional strategies: One size doesn't fit all.* Thousand Oak, CA: Corwin Press.

Gunning, T.G. (2002). *Assessing and correcting reading and writing difficulties.* Boston: Allyn & Bacon.

Harvey, S. & Goudvis, A. (2000). *Strategies that work: Teaching comprehension to enhance under-standing.* Portland, ME: Stenhouse.

Johns, J.L. & Lenski., S.D. (2000). *Improving reading: Strategies and resources.* Dubuque, IA: Kendall-Hunt.

Mather, N., Sammons, J. & Schwartz, J. (2006). Adaptations of the names test: Easy-to-use phonics assessments. *The Reading Teacher, 60,* 114–122. (Freely available online from the International Reading Association archive of articles from The Reading Teacher at www.reading.org)

Professional Literature Cited (continued)

McKenna M.C. & Stahl, S.A. (2003). *Assessment for reading instruction.* New York: Guilford.

McKenna, M.C. & Kear, D.J. (1990). Measuring attitude toward reading: A new tool for teachers. *The Reading Teacher, 43,* 626-639. (Freely available online from the International Reading Association archive of articles from The Reading Teacher at: www.reading.org)

McLaughlin, M. (2002). *Guided comprehension in the primary grades.* Newark, DE: International Reading Association.

Miller, D. (2002). *Reading with Meaning: Teaching comprehension in the primary grades.* Portland, ME: Stenhouse.

Minskoff, E. (2005). *Teaching reading to struggling learners.* Baltimore: Brookes.

Moats, L. 1995. *Spelling: Development, disability and instruction.* Baltimore: York Press.

National Institute of Child Health and Human Development. (2000). *Report of the National Reading Panel. Teaching children to read: An evidence-based assessment of the scientific literature on reading and its implications for reading instruction.* (NIH - 00-4769). Washington, DC: Government Printing Office.

Pearson, P.D. & Gallagher, M.C. (1983). The instruction of reading comprehension. *Contemporary Educational Psychology* 18, 317-344.

Prescott-Griffin, M-L. & Witherell, N.L. (2004). *Fluency in focus.* Portsmouth, NH: Heinemann.

Pressley, M., Allington, R., Wharton-McDonald, R., Block, C. C., & Morrow, L.M. (2001). *Learning to read: Lessons from exemplary first-grade classrooms.* New York: Guilford.

Raphael, T.E., Highfield, K. & Au, K.H. (2006) *QAR now! A powerful and practical framework that develops comprehension and higher-level thinking in all students.* New York: Scholastic.

Rasinski, T. (2003). *The fluent reader.* New York: Scholastic.

Shaywitz, S. (2003). *Overcoming dyslexia: A new and complete science-based program for reading problems at any level.* New York: Vintage.

Strickland, D.S. (2005). *What's after assessment?: Follow-up instruction for phonics, fluency, and comprehension.* Portsmouth, NH: Heinemann.

Strickland, D.S., Ganske, K. & Monroe, J. K. (2002). *Supporting struggling readers and writers: Strategies for classroom intervention.* Portland, ME: Stenhouse.

Tomlinson, C.A. (1999). *The differentiated classroom: Responding to the needs of all learners.* Alexandria, VA: Association for Supervision and Curriculum Development.

Wagstaff, J. (1999). *Teaching reading and writing with word walls.* New York: Scholastic.

Walpole, S. & McKenna, M.C. (2006). The role of informal reading inventories in assessing word recognition. *The Reading Teacher, 59,* 592-594.

Wylie, R. & Durrell, D. (1970). "Teaching Vowels Through Phonograms." *Elementary Education, 47.*